LEITHS HOW TO COOK

BREAD

JENNY STRINGER   CLAIRE MACDONALD
CAMILLA SCHNEIDEMAN

Photography by Peter Cassidy

CONTENTS

NOTES

✳ All spoon measures are level unless otherwise stated:
1 tsp = 5ml spoon; 1 tbsp = 15ml spoon.

✳ Use medium eggs unless otherwise suggested. Anyone who is pregnant or in a vulnerable health group should avoid recipes that use raw egg whites or lightly cooked eggs.

✳ Use fresh herbs unless otherwise suggested.

✳ If using the zest of citrus fruit, buy unwaxed fruit.

✳ Timings are guidelines for conventional ovens. If you are using a fan-assisted oven, set your oven temperature approximately 15°C (1 Gas mark) lower. Use an oven thermometer to check the temperature.

INTRODUCTION

Making your own bread may seem something of a daunting prospect as you read through recipe after recipe that calls for you to leave a dough to rise for 1 hour, 2 hours or even overnight. But don't be put off by lengthy rising times – during most of the bread-making process you are not required to actually do anything. The most complicated of loaves probably will require no more than 30 minutes of activity and the satisfaction of producing your own loaf will feel easily worth the effort.

While there are a few quick breads in this book such as corn or soda bread, the main focus is on how yeast is used to raise a loaf in a near magical way. Understanding what makes yeast work more, or less, efficiently paves the way for hundreds of your own bread creations.

Unlike cake making, it is not the precise weighing of ingredients that guarantees success, but the ability to judge when the dough is ready to be taken on to the next stage, and this book will show you exactly what to look and feel for.

Remember that bread freezes well. If you bake 2 or 3 loaves at a time, you can have a constant supply of home-baked bread to hand. Large loaves can be frozen whole or cut into slices. They should be allowed to cool completely on a wire rack before being well wrapped and put into the freezer. They can be used as soon as they are defrosted, or heated for 10–15 minutes in a medium oven to crisp up the crust again before serving.

GETTING STARTED

KITCHEN TEMPERATURE

The general perception is that bread needs to rise in a warm place, and certainly warmth is needed to activate yeast and get it growing. However, the optimum ambient temperature is around 22°C, which is the temperature of a warm but not oppressively hot kitchen.

Ideally there would be no draughts in the room and the dough would not be placed near intense heat while it rises, as too much heat will kill the yeast. The airing cupboard, where it still exists, has traditionally been thought of as a good place to rise a dough, but your bread will have a better flavour and texture if the dough is left to rise for longer, somewhere cooler.

Bread doughs will happily rise slowly overnight in the fridge; just make sure they are covered and have plenty of room to expand – to avoid opening the fridge door in the morning and finding a blanket of yeasty dough over the whole shelf!

Doughs can also be frozen prior to rising. Simply allow them to defrost at room temperature and they will rise just as a fresh dough would.

The heat of the oven will usually warm an otherwise cool kitchen sufficiently to rise the dough, but on very cold days the flour can be warmed for 5–10 minutes in a low oven before mixing the dough.

EQUIPMENT

THE OVEN

Professional bakers use specialist ovens to achieve the desired crust, flavour and crumb. The most useful function of these ovens is to inject steam at controllable points of the baking process in addition to the steam created naturally by the dough as it bakes. Domestic ovens do not have this function and home bakers sometimes place a tray of hot water on the bottom shelf of the oven before the bread goes in to replicate the steam in the professional baker's oven. These tricks are worth experimenting with, but the effects are limited. Wonderful breads have been made in domestic ovens for centuries and their homemade characteristics should be cherished.

OVEN TEMPERATURE

A dough is risen to its optimum size when it is properly proved, so bread is generally cooked in a very hot oven to stop the yeast working as quickly as possible and prevent the bread 'over-proving'. The air bubbles inside an over-proved loaf are very uneven and the bread tastes very yeasty, having an almost beer-like flavour.

Once the crust has developed and after about half the cooking time, the oven temperature can be reduced in order to cook the dough through properly without burning the crust.

Sweet breads are the exception, as the sugar in the dough means they are often cooked at a lower temperature to prevent burning. Bread can be draped with a loose covering of foil in the oven if it is browning too fast and is not yet cooked inside.

ELECTRIC MIXERS

The recipes in this book describe kneading by hand, as we do not assume everyone has an electric mixer with a dough hook at home. However, the initial kneading of most doughs can be done happily by machine with a dough hook on a low speed to replicate the hand-kneading process. Many bakers then find it satisfying to remove the kneaded dough from the machine and finish it off by hand to make sure the feel of the dough is exactly what they want. While kneading by hand will take up to 10 minutes, kneading by machine should take less than 5 minutes and obviously a lot less of the cook's energy.

Put the dry ingredients into the bowl of the mixer and then add the liquid, making sure you add just enough water to make a soft but not sticky dough. Start on the lowest speed until the ingredients are mixed together and then increase the speed by one notch to knead the dough. The test to see if the dough is sufficiently kneaded is the same as by hand (see page 12).

When using a mixer to knead, it is a good idea to add fragile ingredients that may break up towards the very end of the kneading process, or when you knock back the dough. Raisins and other dried fruit, soft herbs or chunks of chocolate may break up through the dough instead of remaining intact, affecting the appearance, flavour and even the rising time of the bread.

THE TINS

Many people at home use a combination of new metric-sized, as well as older imperial, loaf tins. For this reason we have given a range when specifying tin sizes, as an old 1lb loaf tin works fine for a 500g quantity loaf and a 2lb loaf tin happily bakes a 1kg loaf. The important thing is that the tin is sturdy, and a much loved and used loaf tin will naturally become increasingly non-stick as it ages.

PASTRY SCRAPER

Most of the recipes for yeasted breads in this book will advise you to make a dough that is soft but not sticky. However, a really soft dough will often stick to the work surface and a pastry scraper is the perfect tool to help you get all the dough together after kneading, and to clean the surface at the end.

THE INGREDIENTS

FLOUR

Flour used for baking bread is usually strong wheat flour. The word 'strong' refers to the higher level of the protein gluten found in this flour than in a plain flour used for making pastry or cakes. To make traditionally textured bread with a chewy texture and good crust, gluten must be present.

Strong white flour will give the lightest loaf of all as it has plenty of gluten to make the elastic strands which trap the bubbles created by the yeast, and it doesn't contain any of the grains, wheatgerm or bran found in brown flours which disrupt gluten formation. Brown flours do contain gluten but make a denser loaf than white flour. Mixing the two in varying proportions can mean a good compromise between texture and taste. Granary flour is quite a fine brown flour containing whole grains. This makes a nutty, malty flavoured loaf, with a fairly fine crumb along with its whole grains. Wholemeal flour makes the densest loaves with a malty flavour.

Flour absorbency varies greatly. How much liquid your flour will absorb is party determined by where it has been stored before it even reaches you. A flour that has been stored in very dry conditions will require more water to make a soft dough than a flour that has been stored in a more humid environment. For this reason it is not possible ever to give an absolute water quantity for a recipe; an amount is given as a guide and you must add enough to make a dough of the softness described.

GLUTEN

Gluten is created when the proteins naturally occurring in wheat and many other flours are mixed with liquid and then worked and stretched as the dough is kneaded. When making delicious, crumbly pastry the cook's challenge is to work the dough gently to prevent the gluten developing and making the pastry tough. Here in bread making the opposite is true. Firm energetic kneading will strengthen the gluten, giving the bread the characteristic texture and 'chew' required. When the gluten has been worked sufficiently, the dough looks smooth and is springy and elastic, as opposed to the appearance of the unkneaded dough, which has a rough texture, sometimes described as resembling very acute cellulite!

It is possible to make gluten-free bread, but with gluten absent, some other way must be found to bind the ingredients together, to trap air bubbles and provide some 'chew' in the texture. See pages 50–1 for more information and recipes.

SALT

Salt has more impact on a bread dough than lending flavour. It helps to strengthen the gluten in the flour, so a bread without salt will not only taste bland and stale but also be more cake-like in texture. Salt also helps to give the bread crust its colour.

The basic measurement for salt is 1 level tsp for every 250g flour, although this may vary if other salty ingredients are being added to the dough. Too much salt will slow down the yeast, and your bread may take much longer to rise. Too little and the dough will rise very fast but will have a poor, yeasty flavour.

You can use normal table salt in bread, although many people prefer to use the larger flaked sea salt as it contains other minerals and has a more complex flavour. However, these larger flakes are a little harder to distribute throughout the dough, so they are better ground down a little before being added to the flour, or dissolved in the liquid used in the recipe.

YEAST

Yeast is a living substance, a single-celled organism of the fungus family. Like most other living things it needs food, warmth and moisture to grow and, as it grows, it gives off carbon dioxide bubbles. So if the yeast is distributed evenly throughout the dough, and its food and moisture also dispersed evenly, it should give off its bubbles of gas evenly too, and the final loaf should have a uniform, light texture from the network of bubbles.

Excess heat will kill yeast, and an excess of salt or very cold surroundings will slow it down. Fresh yeast can be stored, well wrapped in the fridge for at least several days, sometimes much longer (check the sell-by date) or frozen (again closely wrapped) for up to 1 month. Yeast that has been frozen for longer than this will still work but may be less effective, so it is a good idea to increase the quantity by a quarter.

The two types of yeast we use at Leiths are fresh yeast and fast-action dried yeast. Both work well to produce great bread, and part of choosing which to use for a recipe comes down to personal preference. A recipe using fresh yeast can also be made with fast-action (also sometimes known as easy-blend) dried yeast. As a general rule, you will need four times as much fresh yeast as you will fast-action dried yeast to achieve the same rise. So if a recipe calls for 20g fresh yeast, you will only need 5g fast-action dried.

The quantity of yeast needed will vary according to the other ingredients in the dough. Doughs containing fat, nuts and sugar will need more yeast to rise than a plain dough made of only flour, water and a little salt. However, the basic guideline is that 10g fresh yeast will rise a plain dough made with 250g flour.

When using fresh yeast, place it in a small bowl, add a little of the warm liquid from the recipe and stir to dissolve the yeast; it is then easily distributed through the flour. Traditionally, the yeast liquid would be left to stand until frothing (this is known as sponging the yeast) before being added to the flour. This was done to check that the yeast was fresh and still active. These days you can expect yeast sold commercially to work, and so only need to sponge it if you have been keeping it for a while and are worried that it has gone stale, or if it has been frozen.

Fast-action dried yeast is stirred into the flour along with any other dry ingredients, and then the liquid is added and mixed to make the dough, which is a little quicker than using fresh yeast. This type of yeast is also very reliable and powerful and so a good bread can be made with it even after kneading and rising only once. A level tsp fast-action dried yeast weighs about 2.3g.

FAT
Bread can be made without any fat at all, but will stale more quickly than bread made with some fat in its ingredients. Fat will give the bread a softer texture and will help the crust turn golden brown. Butter or a well-flavoured olive oil will influence the taste of a loaf as well as making the dough easier to knead.

The usual quantity of fat for a basic loaf would be 20–30g for 250g flour. Any more than this and the fat will make the yeast sluggish and the softening effect on the gluten in the flour will result in more of a cake-like texture to the bread. This is actually a desirable characteristic in many enriched doughs, such as brioche (see page 106).

LIQUID
The old adage 'the wetter the dough the better the dough' applies. The best bread doughs are those that are as soft as they can be while still just firm enough to knead. They will yield loaves of the most delectable texture once they are cooked.

The ideal temperature of the liquid is about 37–38°C, which we call warm or tepid: when you put your finger in, it will feel just warm. It is sometimes referred to as blood temperature (an out-dated culinary term!). Liquid that is just warm will get the yeast working at once and speed the process a little without adversely affecting the flavour of the final loaf. Water that is too hot will actually kill the yeast and stop it working altogether.

Water on its own will make a loaf with a rustic, open texture and a strong crust, while the fat content of milk will make softer, finer loaves. Again, due to the increased fat content, a milk loaf will stale more slowly than bread made with only water.

Most recipes using milk rather than water call for the milk to be scalded and then cooled to tepid before being added to the dough. This may feel like a waste of time, heating a liquid only to cool it again, but unless milk has been heated to steaming temperature, the milk proteins stop the gluten in the flour becoming properly elastic. This may be an advantage when making soft, cake-like doughs, but should be avoided in bread. The cooling down of the milk to tepid can be speeded up by pouring it from the pan into a large cold bowl. It's not that bread can't be made with unscalded milk, it is just that cooled, scalded milk makes a well-textured bread more easily. To scald milk, heat it until on the verge of boiling, with steam escaping and bubbles starting to form around the edge of the pan.

Beer is frequently used in wholemeal or brown breads and lends a depth of flavour. However, it must be boiled (to drive off the alcohol) and then cooled or the alcohol in the beer will affect the yeast's growth.

Occasionally vinegar and other acidic liquids are added to bread doughs to help develop the gluten and give some hint of the flavour of a sourdough-type loaf.

It is wise to start by adding at least three quarters of the liquid quantity called for in a bread recipe and then adding as much of the remaining quarter as necessary to create a dough of the correct softness. Do bear in mind that it is preferable – and much easier – to add a little extra flour to correct a dough that is too sticky than to add extra liquid to a dough once it has been mixed.

OTHER ADDED INGREDIENTS
Flavouring ingredients – like nuts, seeds, grated cheeses, herbs or dried fruit – are best added to the dough after it has risen the first time, as if they are added at the beginning they can slow the bread's rise and break up the dough. Either knead them in while knocking back the dough, or roll the dough out after it has had its first rise, scatter the addition over the surface, roll it up like a Swiss roll and then continue to knead until well distributed.

Purées of potatoes or other vegetables or cooked rice can be added to help bread stay moist for longer, such as the sesame bread on page 38 and sweet potato rolls on page 72.

Sweetness can be added in different ways, with white or brown sugar, maple syrup or honey for flavour.

THE STAGES OF BREAD MAKING

To make most yeast-risen breads you simply follow the steps described below and illustrated in detail overleaf. Nothing will go dramatically wrong if a dough has to wait a little before being taken on to the next stage, so make your bread dough fit in with your schedule and not the other way round. As with any rule there are always the exceptions. There may be steps missed out in particular recipes; for example where it is desirable to have a loaf with rustic, uneven holes in the crumb, there is no need for a second kneading to even out the bubbles in the dough, but it is a good idea to learn the usual stages of bread making as many loaves rely on this traditional process.

The acronym we sometimes use at Leiths to help our students remember the stages in order is: 'Mary knits red knickers pretty badly' but feel free to create your own!

MIXING
This initial stage combines the ingredients evenly and gives you the opportunity to add more liquid or flour to ensure your dough is soft but not too sticky right from the start.

KNEADING
A vigorous kneading develops (or strengthens) the gluten present in the flour, which is necessary for the 'chew' of a good bread texture. (The cooked elastic dough of bread is described as having a 'chew' as you eat it as opposed to the tender soft crumb of a cooked cake mixture.) Also, kneading distributes the yeast and any other added ingredients evenly throughout the dough. Kneading can be done by hand or machine and usually takes less than 10 minutes. To test if the dough is kneaded sufficiently, pull it into a tight ball and press with your finger; it should spring back as the gluten will have become elastic.

RISING
Leaving the kneaded dough alone to rest allows the yeast to grow and multiply, producing carbon dioxide bubbles which cause the dough to rise. Most doughs should double in size at this stage, and rising may take between 1 and 2 hours for a classic loaf at slightly warm room temperature. Doughs that

rise much faster than this tend to do so because they have too much yeast in them or the room temperature is too warm, and the flavour will be impaired. In a cold room a dough will rise slowly but the flavour will not be compromised, and in some cases will actually improve. Rising times are given as a guide only, as they may vary considerably. If you are in any doubt, slightly over-rising rather than under-rising a loaf is preferable.

KNOCKING BACK
This involves knocking the large air bubbles out of the risen dough and kneading it again, usually for just 2–3 minutes, to create an even-textured crumb. This is also the stage at which ingredients such as dried fruit, nuts or herbs can be added.

SHAPING
After knocking back the dough is shaped into a loaf (or loaves) or rolls. A loaf can take many forms, from a simple tin loaf or freeform round to a plait. It is important to shape the loaf properly, as a well-shaped loaf will have an even crust.

PROVING
This second rising of the dough, in its designated shape, will normally take around half the time of the first rising. The yeast makes the dough rise again, with a finer network of bubbles. It is proved when it is nearly at its final size and you can tell by not only its bulk but also by touch. It should feel soft and pillowy and when you press the dough with your finger (somewhere the indent will not show too much) it will only spring back a little. Most of the breads in this book are proved covered with lightly oiled cling film. It is really important that you remember to oil the cling film, or as you gently remove it, the dough can collapse or its beautifully smooth surface be pulled away.

BAKING
Bread is baked at a high temperature to kill the yeast and set the shape of the loaf quickly. Most breads are done when they are golden brown, feel light for their size and sound hollow when tapped on the base.

KNEADING BY HAND

1 On the work surface, use the bottom of the palm of one hand to push the dough away from you diagonally.

2 Then reverse the movement, rolling the dough back with the fingertips of the same hand.

3 Repeat with the other hand, so the dough is moving diagonally in front of you in the other direction. Continue to knead in this way, alternating between hands, until the dough feels smooth and elastic.

4 Shape the dough into a ball in the hands, creating a smooth, fairly taut surface, and press it with your finger. If it bounces at least three quarters of the way back and shows some elasticity, it has been kneaded sufficiently.

RISING

1 Place the kneaded dough in a very lightly oiled bowl, cover the bowl with lightly oiled cling film and place in a warm (but not hot), draught-free place to rise for about an hour or as suggested in the recipe.

2 When the dough is well risen, to at least twice its original volume, remove the cling film from the bowl.

KNOCKING BACK

1 Turn the risen dough out of the bowl onto the work surface, ready to knock back (i.e. knead for a second time).

2 Knead the dough in the same way as before to deflate it and break down and distribute all the large air bubbles created by the yeast during rising. This should only take 2–3 minutes.

SHAPING
Shape the dough into a round and pull it around on itself.

2 Continue to pull the dough around on itself to tighten it.

3 Continue to shape in this way to give the dough a smooth, taut surface, then roll it a little, smooth side down.

4 Place the dough neatly, smooth side uppermost, in the prepared loaf tin.

PROVING

Leave the dough to prove or rise again in the tin, covered lightly with cling film, until risen by at least half its size again. Check the dough: if it springs back fully when it is lightly pressed it needs to be proved for longer.

2 The dough is ready to bake when it is lightly pressed and the indentation remains, springing back only a little.

BAKING

To check if the baked loaf is ready, tap it on the underside with the knuckles: it should sound hollow. If it doesn't, return the loaf to the tin and oven and continue to cook a little longer.

BREAD FINISHES AND GLAZES

There are various ways to enhance the appearance of the crust, the simplest being a dusting of flour before baking, which gives a rustic, natural and soft finish.

For shine and a rich colour, you can brush the top of the loaf with sieved beaten egg before baking and sprinkle with seeds if you like, too.

A milk glaze will give a softer crust and matt finish. Liquid glazes should be applied very thinly, using a pastry brush. Avoid any dripping to the edges, as this can cause the bread to stick to the tin.

You can also slash the top of the bread to give an attractive rustic appearance, either before the bread proves (the slashes open and expand while proving and even more when baking), or 10–15 minutes before baking so they open up a little. Use a very sharp knife or single sided razor blade to make shallow cuts in the dough.

To achieve a very soft crust, keep the loaf covered with a tea towel as it cools.

GLAZING Brushing the loaf with beaten egg for a shiny finish.

SLASHING Scoring the surface of the proved dough on the diagonal with a sharp knife to create slashes, which will open up a little during baking.

BAKING Dusting the surface of the dough with flour for a rustic finish.

1

LARGE LOAVES

The sense of pride engendered by bringing a loaf to the table
is one of the great pleasures of life. Here you will find classic
tin loaves, rustic round loaves, plaits and oil-rich tray loaves,
made using different flours and a variety of added flavourings.

All of the breads in this chapter are destined to be shared –
thinly sliced, ripped apart, slathered with butter or dipped into
pungent olive oil. No matter how we eat them, we love our
daily bread, and so much the better if the evocative smell
of baking still lingers in the air.

WHITE BREAD

MAKES 1 small loaf

250g strong white flour, plus extra to dust
1 tsp salt
15–20g salted butter or sunflower oil, plus oil to grease

100–150ml tepid water
10g fresh yeast
1 egg, to glaze (optional)

You will need a 450–500g loaf tin.

1 Mix the flour and salt in a bowl. Rub in the butter, if using, with your fingertips. In a small bowl, mix 2 tbsp of the tepid water with the yeast, to create a loose paste. Add the yeast to the flour, splash a little more of the water into the yeast bowl, swirl it around and pour into the flour to ensure no yeast is lost. Add three quarters of the remaining water, with the oil if using, and mix using a cutlery knife to distribute the water.

2 Add the remaining water, if necessary. It is important that there is enough water to make a soft dough, so feel it. If not enough water is added, the dough will be dry and firm, difficult to knead and will make a dry loaf. The dough should be tacky, but not too sticky to work with.

3 Knead the dough on the work surface for 5–8 minutes, using the bottom of the palm of one hand to push the dough away from you diagonally, then rolling it back with the fingertips of the same hand. Repeat with the other hand, so the dough is moving diagonally in front of you, alternating between hands. Avoid adding flour even if the dough sticks to the surface a little; only sprinkle it with flour if it is very sticky and making kneading difficult.

4 After about 5 minutes of kneading, shape the dough in your hands, creating a smooth, fairly taut surface, and press it with your finger. If it bounces at least three quarters of the way back and shows some elasticity, it will have been kneaded sufficiently. If it doesn't bounce back or only a very little, it requires more kneading.

5 Place the kneaded dough in a very lightly oiled bowl, cover with lightly oiled cling film or a damp tea towel and place in a warm (but not hot), draught-free place for about 1 hour, to rise and double in size. Lightly oil the loaf tin.

6 Once doubled in size, remove the dough from the bowl and knock it back, by kneading for 2–3 minutes in the same way as before, to break down and distribute all the large bubbles created by the yeast during rising.

7 Shape the dough by pulling it around on itself to create a smooth, taut surface and roll it a little, smooth side down, on the work surface. Place it neatly, smooth side uppermost, in the prepared loaf tin and cover with lightly oiled cling film. Prove the dough (allow it to rise again) by at least half its size again. Meanwhile, heat the oven to 200°C/gas mark 6.

8 After about 30 minutes, check the dough: it is ready to bake when it is lightly pressed and the indentation remains, springing back only a little. If it springs back fully then continue to prove for longer. If using an egg glaze, lightly beat the egg, using a fork, then sieve it.

9 Brush the loaf gently with the egg glaze or dust with flour and bake in the top third of the oven for 25–30 minutes. Open the oven door when the bread smells cooked; it should be golden. Remove the bread and invert from the tin using oven gloves. It should feel light, and when tapped on the underside should sound hollow. If not, return the loaf to the tin and oven and continue to cook a little longer. Allow the cooked loaf to cool completely on a wire rack.

1 Mixing the water into the dough, using a cutlery knife.

2 Checking the consistency of the dough; it should feel tacky but not too wet.

3 Kneading the dough until it feels smooth and elastic.

4 Shaping the dough into a ball with a smooth, taut surface.

(Continued overleaf)

5 The dough having risen to double its size.

6 Kneading the dough vigorously to knock it back and produce a more even texture.

7 Placing the dough in the lightly oiled loaf tin, ready to prove.

8 Checking the dough by pressing lightly with a finger; it is ready if it leaves a little indentation.

WHOLEMEAL BREAD

MAKES 2 small loaves

300–350ml milk
20g fresh yeast
1 tsp caster sugar
50g butter
250g wholemeal flour

250g strong plain white flour,
  plus extra to dust
2 tsp salt
Oil, to grease

This wholemeal bread uses a mixture of white and wholemeal flour so it has a lovely light texture, along with the malty flavour of a traditional brown loaf. This recipe makes 2 loaves, so pop one in the freezer. You could even slice it before freezing for a ready supply of toast! You will need two 450–500g loaf tins.

1 Pour the milk into a small saucepan, bring to scalding point (see page 155) over a medium heat, then remove from the heat. Set aside to allow the milk to cool to tepid, about 38°C.

2 Put the yeast and sugar into a small bowl, add 2 tbsp of the tepid milk and stir to dissolve.

3 Cut the butter into small dice, add to the remaining tepid milk and leave to melt.

4 Put the flours and salt in a large bowl. Add the yeast mixture and about three quarters of the milk and butter mixture, trying to ensure all the butter is added. Using a cutlery knife, distribute the liquid evenly and bring together into a soft dough, adding the remaining milk and butter as needed. When the dough is beginning to form, use your hands to bring it together.

5 Transfer to a very lightly floured work surface and knead for 5–8 minutes (see page 12) until smooth and elastic.

6 Put the dough in a large, lightly oiled bowl and cover lightly with oiled cling film. Leave to rise in a warm place for about 1 hour until doubled in size.

7 Transfer the dough to the work surface and knock it back, kneading it for 2–3 minutes. Lightly oil the loaf tins.

8 Divide the dough in half, shape into 2 loaves (see page 14) and place in the prepared loaf tins. Cover with lightly oiled cling film and leave to prove in a warm, but not too hot, place. Meanwhile, heat the oven to 200°C/gas mark 6.

9 To check the dough has proved enough, lightly press it in one corner with your finger; it should leave only a little indentation. Sprinkle flour over the tops of the loaves and bake in the oven for 25–30 minutes until browned. Turn one of the loaves onto a wire rack; it should feel light and sound hollow when tapped on the underside. If not, return to the oven to cook for a further 5 minutes. Remove the loaves from the tins and leave to cool on a wire rack.

Variation

✳ **Wholemeal seeded loaf** Knead in 5 tbsp mixed seeds such as poppy, sesame, sunflower or millet seeds when you knock back the dough in step 7.

A note on using wholemeal flour...

✳ You can use all wholemeal flour for this bread, but be aware that the greater the proportion of wholemeal to white flour, the heavier and denser the loaf will be. We don't use strong wholemeal flour, as ordinary wholemeal gives a softer loaf, but you can use strong wholemeal if you prefer.

ENRICHED WHITE BREAD

MAKES 2 small loaves	
300–350ml milk	500g strong plain flour,
30g butter	plus extra to dust
20g fresh yeast	2 tsp salt
1 tsp caster sugar	2 eggs
	Oil, to grease

This loaf has a soft, tender crumb and is perfect for making sandwiches, toasting, or serving with soup. The dough also makes delicious dinner rolls (see page 66). You will need two 450–500g loaf tins.

1 Put the milk in a small saucepan and bring to scalding point (see page 155) over a medium heat. Remove from the heat, transfer 2 tbsp to a small bowl and set aside to cool to tepid, about 38°C. Cut the butter into small dice and add to the remaining milk in the pan. Leave to melt and cool to tepid.

2 Add the yeast and sugar to the cooled milk in the bowl and stir until dissolved.

3 Put the flour and salt into a large bowl.

4 Break an egg into a small bowl, beat lightly and add to the flour, along with the yeast mixture and at least three quarters of the milk and butter mixture (using some of it to swill out any remaining yeast in its bowl). Use a cutlery knife to distribute the liquid evenly and bring the ingredients together into a dough. Add more milk and butter if necessary to create a soft, slightly tacky dough.

5 When the dough is beginning to form, use your hands to bring it together. Transfer to a very lightly floured surface and knead for 5–8 minutes (see page 12) until smooth and elastic.

6 Put the dough into a large, very lightly oiled bowl, cover with lightly oiled cling film and leave to rise in a warm place for about 1 hour until doubled in size.

7 Transfer the risen dough to the work surface and knock it back, kneading it for 2–3 minutes. Lightly oil the loaf tins.

8 Divide the dough in half, shape into 2 loaves (see page 14) and place in the prepared loaf tins. Cover with oiled cling film and leave to prove in a warm place until risen by at least half their size again. Meanwhile, heat the oven to 200°C/gas mark 6.

9 To check the dough has proved enough, lightly press it in one corner with your finger; it should leave only a little indentation. Whisk the other egg with a fork, sieve it and use to brush the risen loaves. Bake in the top third of the oven for 25–30 minutes until golden. Turn the bread onto a wire rack; it should feel light and sound hollow when tapped on the underside. If not, return the bread to the oven to cook for a further 5 minutes. Leave to cool on a wire rack.

A note on enriching doughs...

✳ Adding fats in the form of butter, oil or egg yolk, or adding sugar, alcohol or spices to a bread dough affects the way the yeast and the gluten work. The gluten strands won't be as strong, so the bread will have a softer, more cake-like texture. The yeast will also work more slowly, so the process will take longer. Often enriched dough bread recipes use a little more yeast to counterbalance these effects. If the liquid used is milk rather than water, it is heated to scalding point to destroy an enzyme that interferes with gluten, then cooled to the right temperature before mixing.

CRUNCHY SEEDED GRANARY PLAIT

MAKES 1 large plaited loaf	
150ml whole milk	1 tsp salt
55g butter	2 eggs
2 tsp Marmite (optional)	Oil, to grease
150ml buttermilk	2 tbsp sunflower seeds
20g fresh yeast	2 tbsp golden linseeds
1 tsp caster sugar	1 tbsp pumpkin seeds
225g granary flour	1 tbsp flax seeds
225g strong white flour,	1 tbsp chia seeds
plus extra to dust	1 tbsp poppy seeds, to finish

Don't feel daunted by the prospect of using unusual seeds, and in such volume. The idea of this loaf is to provide as much crunchy texture and toasty, nutty flavour as possible, from a good variety of seeds. Experiment with the seed mix until you find your favourite combination. Marmite may seem an unlikely addition, but it lends a satisfyingly savoury flavour. You can use a mixture of milk and plain yoghurt in place of the buttermilk.

1 Pour the milk into a small saucepan and bring to scalding point (see page 155) over a medium heat. Remove from the heat, transfer 2 tbsp to a small bowl and set aside to cool to tepid, about 38°C.

2 Cut the butter into small dice and add to the milk in the pan. Add the Marmite, if using, and stir until melted, then leave to cool until tepid. Stir in the buttermilk. Add the yeast and sugar to the tepid milk in the small bowl and stir to dissolve.

3 Mix the flours and salt in a large bowl. Break one of the eggs into a small bowl, beat lightly and add to the flour, along with the yeast mixture and the milk and Marmite mixture. Use a cutlery knife to distribute the liquid evenly and bring the ingredients together into a dough. When the dough is beginning to form, use your hands to bring it together.

4 Turn onto a lightly floured surface and knead for 5–8 minutes (see page 12) until smooth and elastic. Put the dough in a very lightly oiled bowl, cover with lightly oiled cling film and leave to rise in a warm place until doubled in size, about 1 hour.

5 Transfer the risen dough back to the work surface and pat it out with the palm of your hand into a rough disc. Scatter all the seeds, except the poppy seeds, over the dough, leaving a clear margin, then gather the edges to encase the seeds.

6 Knock back the dough by kneading until the seeds are distributed evenly throughout the dough, about 1–2 minutes.

7 Divide the dough into 3 equal pieces and shape into a plait (as shown overleaf). Place the plait on a lightly oiled baking sheet, cover with lightly oiled cling film and leave to prove in a warm place until risen to at least half its size again, and if you press the dough lightly with your finger, it leaves only a small indentation. Meanwhile, heat the oven to 200°C/gas mark 6.

8 Beat the remaining egg with a fork and sieve it. Brush the risen plaited loaf with the beaten egg and sprinkle over the poppy seeds.

9 Bake in the top third of the oven for 25–30 minutes until golden, then transfer to a wire rack; it should feel light for its size and sound hollow when tapped on the underside. If not, return to the oven to cook for a further 5 minutes, upside down. Leave to cool on a wire rack.

Variation

✳ **Seeded cob** Rather than shape the loaf into a plait, you can simply form it into a tight ball. Flatten it slightly on the oiled baking sheet before glazing and baking as above.

STEP 3 Mixing the liquid ingredients into the combined flours and salt, using a cutlery knife.

STEP 4 Kneading the dough until it is smooth and elastic.

STEP 5 Scattering the mixed seeds over risen dough.

STEP 6 Kneading the dough to knock it back and distribute the seeds evenly.

(Continued overleaf)

SHAPING A PLAIT

1 Place 2 strands of dough parallel to each other and 2.5cm apart. Put the third one across the middle of them, threading it under the left-hand piece and over the right-hand piece.

2 Starting from the middle and working towards one end, plait the strands, taking the left-hand piece and placing it over the right-hand piece, then the right over the left.

3 Continue in this way to plait the pieces together until you reach the end, then repeat to plait the other end.

4 Tuck the ends of the strands under the plait to neaten.

FARMHOUSE LOAF

MAKES 1 large loaf

20g fresh yeast
200–250ml tepid water
1 tsp soft dark brown sugar
1 tbsp olive oil, plus extra
   to grease

200g strong white flour,
   plus extra to dust
200g strong wholemeal flour
1½ tsp salt
1 tbsp malt vinegar

Inspired by Elizabeth David's experiments in baking, this loaf is baked on a baking sheet under a deep, heavy casserole which mimics the effect of a steamy commercial bread oven and gives the loaf an extra boost in the oven as it rises to almost fill the casserole. Requiring only one rising, it is also quicker to make than most yeast breads. You will need a deep, round, 23–25cm Le Creuset-style casserole.

1 Put the yeast, 2–3 tbsp of the water and the sugar in a small bowl and stir to dissolve. Lightly flour a baking sheet and oil the inside of the casserole.

2 Combine the flours and salt in a large bowl. Add the yeast mixture, swilling out the bowl with a little more of the water to ensure all the yeast is incorporated, then add the oil, vinegar and enough of the remaining water to make a soft but not sticky dough.

3 Knead for 8–10 minutes (see page 12) until smooth and elastic, then shape the dough into a smooth ball.

4 Place on the floured baking sheet and press down slightly. Brush with oil, cover with the upturned casserole and leave to prove in a warm place for 1½–2 hours, or until it leaves only a little indentation when you lightly press the corner of the dough with your finger. Meanwhile, heat the oven to 220°C/ gas mark 7.

5 Transfer to the oven and bake for 30–45 minutes, then take out and carefully remove the casserole, using oven gloves, and test the loaf. The base should sound hollow when tapped. If the bread is not yet cooked, or the crust is too pale, return it to the oven without the casserole, for about 15 minutes. Leave to cool on a wire rack before slicing.

GRANT LOAF

MAKES 1 large loaf

15g fresh yeast
600ml tepid water
1 tbsp runny honey
675g stoneground organic
   wholemeal flour

2 tsp sea salt
Oil, to grease

Doris Grant invented this recipe during the war to encourage people to bake their own bread. It relies on really fresh yeast and good quality wholemeal flour. The loaf keeps well, the flavour improving after a day or two. It has quite a dense texture but it is delicious, and quick and easy to make – from start to finish in just an hour. You will need a 900g–1kg loaf tin.

1 In a small bowl, mix together the yeast, a little of the water and the honey. Leave to stand for 10 minutes until frothy (this will assure you that the yeast is alive and active).

2 Mix the flour and salt in a large bowl and make a well in the centre. Add the yeast mixture to the well and enough of the water to make a soft dough. Take care when adding the water as this dough can easily become too wet. Mix the dough vigorously with your hands for about 2 minutes until it leaves the sides of the bowl. Lightly oil the loaf tin.

3 Place the dough in the prepared loaf tin, smooth the surface with your fingers, then cover with lightly oiled cling film and leave to rise in a warm place until it reaches the top of the tin, about 30–40 minutes. Meanwhile, heat the oven to 200°C/ gas mark 6.

4 Bake in the oven for 40–50 minutes, or until the loaf sounds hollow when tapped on the underside. Turn out onto a wire rack and leave to cool before slicing.

BEER BREAD

MAKES 1 small loaf

30g butter
1 tsp soft light brown sugar
175ml brown ale
10g fresh yeast
1 tbsp tepid water

125g wholemeal flour
125g strong plain white flour,
    plus extra to dust
1 tsp salt
1 small egg

This bread is perfect to enjoy with cheese, for a simple ploughman's lunch, or served in chunks with a hearty soup or stew. You will need a 450–500g loaf tin.

1 Use a little of the butter to grease the loaf tin, then put the remainder in a small saucepan with the sugar and ale. Place over a medium to high heat, stir to melt the sugar and butter into the liquid, then bring to the boil. Remove from the heat and leave to cool to tepid.

2 Put the yeast in a bowl, add the tepid water and mix to a loose paste.

3 Sift the flours and salt into a large bowl. Reserve 1 tsp of the bran from the sieve for the top of the loaf and tip the rest into the bowl with the flours.

4 Break the egg into a small bowl and beat lightly, then add it to the flours. Add the yeast mixture and three quarters of the ale and butter mixture. Mix first with a cutlery knife and then with your fingers, adding enough of the reserved ale mixture to make a soft but not sticky dough.

5 Turn out onto a very lightly floured surface and knead for about 5–8 minutes (see page 12) until smooth and elastic, using as little extra flour as possible on the work surface to stop the dough sticking.

6 Place the dough in a very lightly oiled bowl and cover with lightly oiled cling film or a damp tea towel. Leave in a warm place until doubled in size, about 1 hour.

7 Transfer the risen dough to the work surface and knock it back, kneading it for 2–3 minutes. Lightly oil the loaf tin.

8 Shape the dough into a loaf (see page 14) and place smooth side up in the prepared loaf tin. Cover with lightly oiled cling film and leave to prove until risen by at least half its size again. Meanwhile, heat the oven to 200°C/gas mark 6.

9 Sprinkle the reserved bran over the top of the loaf and bake in the oven for 30–40 minutes, or until golden brown and it feels light and sounds hollow when tapped on the bottom. Remove from the tin and leave to cool on a wire rack.

A note on using beer...

✻ Beer lends a unique, slightly sour taste to bread. The darker beer you use, the darker the bread and the stronger the flavour of the bread will be.

Variation

✻ **Rosemary and fig bread** Replace the ale with 175ml milk, brought to scalding point (see page 155) and cooled to tepid before using. Knead 200g sliced dried figs and 1 tbsp roughly chopped rosemary into the dough when knocking it back, then shape the dough as a round or oval loaf on an oiled baking sheet. Place olive oil soaked sprigs of rosemary on top before baking (as for focaccia, see page 44) and drizzle with a little honey when it first comes out of the oven.

OAT LOAF

60g porridge oats, plus
   1 tbsp for the top
150ml boiling water
1 orange
100ml buttermilk or
   natural yoghurt
1½ tbsp runny honey

300g strong white flour
7g fast-action dried yeast
1 tsp salt
100–150ml tepid water
Oil, to grease
1 egg

For this loaf oats are made into a porridge-like mix, which keeps the bread moist, even though the only added fat comes from the buttermilk or yoghurt. If you are making small loaves, freeze one of them, ready sliced, for breakfast toast whenever you need it. You will need one 1kg or two 450–500g loaf tins.

1 Put the oats in a bowl, pour on the boiling water and stir well. Leave to soak and to cool to tepid.

2 Finely grate the zest of half the orange and stir into the buttermilk or yoghurt with the honey.

3 Put the flour into a large bowl and stir in the yeast, then the salt. Stir in the soaked oats, the buttermilk mixture and enough of the tepid water to make a soft but not sticky dough (bearing in mind that the oats release a lot of liquid, so it may seem like you need more water than you actually do).

4 Knead for 10 minutes (see page 12) until smooth and elastic. Place in a lightly oiled bowl and cover with lightly oiled cling film. Leave in a warm place for 1 hour, or until the dough has doubled in size.

5 Quickly knock back the dough and knead for a couple of minutes, or until the larger air bubbles seem to have been kneaded out. Lightly oil the loaf tin(s).

6 If using small tins, divide the dough into 2 even pieces. Shape the dough into one large or two small loaves (see page 14) and place smooth side up in the prepared loaf tin(s). Cover with lightly oiled cling film and leave to prove for 45–60 minutes, or until nearly doubled in size, and if you press the corner with your finger, it leaves an indent. Meanwhile, heat the oven to 220°C/gas mark 7.

7 In a small bowl, beat the egg using a fork, and then sieve it. Lightly brush the top of the dough with the beaten egg and sprinkle with the porridge oats.

8 Bake in the top third of the oven for 20 minutes, then lower the oven setting to 200°C/gas mark 6 and move the loaf tin(s) down to the middle shelf. Cook for a further 20–25 minutes, covering loosely with foil if the surface browns too much before the bread is cooked. When cooked, remove from the tin(s) and cool on a wire rack.

Variation

✳ Apricot and oat loaf For a delicious fruit loaf add 150g chopped ready-to-eat dried apricots with the oats before you pour on the boiling water.

PUMPKIN BREAD

MAKES 1 medium loaf

100g pumpkin seeds
Oil, to grease
100–150ml tepid water
20g fresh yeast
1 tsp caster sugar

450g strong white flour,
    plus extra to dust
2 tsp salt
1 egg, beaten
200g tin pumpkin purée
2 tbsp runny honey

This handsome, tasty loaf is particularly good served warm from the oven with cheese. You can, of course, make your own pumpkin purée by cooking chunks of pumpkin with a little water in a covered pan until soft, and then puréeing it in a food processor or blender.

1 Heat a dry frying pan over a medium heat and lightly toast the pumpkin seeds, then transfer them to a plate to cool. Lightly oil a large baking sheet.

2 In a small bowl, mix 2 tbsp of the tepid water with the yeast to create a loose paste. Mix in the sugar.

3 Sift the flour and salt into a large bowl. Make a well in the centre and add the egg, yeast mixture and pumpkin purée. Add enough of the remaining water (start with three quarters) to mix to a soft dough, using a little to swill out the yeast bowl to make sure none is left behind.

4 Turn the dough out onto a lightly floured surface and knead until smooth and elastic (see page 12), up to 10 minutes. Place in a lightly oiled bowl, cover with oiled cling film and leave to rise in a warm place until doubled in size, about 45–60 minutes.

5 Tip the dough out onto a lightly floured surface and flatten it out with your hands. Sprinkle over the seeds and knead again until it is smooth and the seeds are evenly distributed.

6 Shape into a domed circle and place on the oiled baking sheet. Cover with oiled cling film and leave to prove for about 30 minutes, or until increased in size by half. Meanwhile, heat the oven to 220°C/gas mark 7.

7 Slash the top of the bread using a large, sharp knife and bake for 30–45 minutes, turning the oven setting down slightly to 200°C/gas mark 6 after 5 minutes. It is ready when the crust is well browned, and the loaf feels light for its size and sounds hollow when tapped on the underside.

8 Transfer the loaf to a wire rack, brush with the honey while still warm and leave to cool a little before serving.

SESAME BREAD

MAKES 1 large loaf

85g jasmine rice
15g fresh yeast
250ml tepid water
500g strong white flour,
    plus extra to dust

2 tsp salt
50g sesame seeds
1 tbsp olive oil, plus extra
    to grease

This loaf has the unusual addition of cooked rice, which keeps it very moist, and as the dough is so soft, it requires hardly any kneading. The recipe calls for jasmine rice but in fact any rice can be used. Leftover cooked rice (about 250g) could even be reheated in a microwave and incorporated into the dough, but must be reheated until piping hot, then cooled to warm.

1 Cook the rice in a small saucepan until soft, according to the packet instructions (not al dente, as you might to eat with a curry), then drain and leave in the sieve to cool until warm.

2 Meanwhile, put the yeast in a small bowl and stir in 2–3 tbsp of the tepid water to dissolve.

3 Mix the flour and salt in a large bowl and stir in the sesame seeds. Now add the warm rice, mixing well. Stir in the yeast, swilling out the yeast bowl with some of the water, then stir in the oil and enough of the remaining water to make a soft dough, using a cutlery knife or wooden spoon.

4 Cover with lightly oiled cling film and leave the dough to rise in a warm place for 1–1½ hours until doubled in size.

5 Give the dough a light knead in the bowl (it will be too soft to knead in a traditional way). Then, with floured hands, shape it into a ball and elongate 2 ends using your fingers, to make a rugby ball shape. Place on an oiled baking sheet.

6 Cover with lightly oiled cling film and leave to prove until it has increased in size by half again, and if you press the corner with your finger, it leaves an indent. Meanwhile, heat the oven to 220°C/gas mark 7.

7 Sift a little flour over the dough and bake in the oven for 15 minutes, then lower the oven setting to 200°C/gas mark 6 and cook for a further 20–30 minutes. The loaf should feel light for its size and sound hollow when tapped on the base. Cool on a wire rack.

POTATO BREAD WITH CARAWAY AND ONION SEED

MAKES 1 large loaf	
350g strong white flour, plus extra to dust	2 tsp caraway seeds
50g rye flour	1 tsp malt vinegar
1½ tsp salt	250ml tepid water
7g fast-action dried yeast	50g mashed potato
1 tsp black onion seeds	Oil, to grease

The unusual addition of potato keeps this loaf lovely and moist. With the distinctive flavours of caraway and rye, this is the perfect sandwich loaf for pastrami or other cured meats, and strong cheeses such as Gruyère. You will need a 900g–1kg loaf tin.

1 Mix the flours and salt in a large bowl and stir in the yeast, onion seeds and caraway seeds.

2 Stir the vinegar and enough of the tepid water (about 75ml) into the potato to make a pourable mixture, and pour into the flour. Add enough of the remaining water to make a soft but not sticky dough.

3 Knead the dough on a work surface for about 2 minutes (see page 12) until smooth. Put the dough in a lightly oiled bowl, cover with lightly oiled cling film and leave to rise until doubled in size, 1–2 hours.

4 Knock the dough back and knead for a couple of minutes. Lightly oil the loaf tin.

5 Shape the dough to fit into the prepared tin (see page 14) and cover loosely with lightly oiled cling film. Leave to prove until increased in size by half, and if you press the corner lightly with your finger, it leaves only a shallow indentation. Meanwhile, heat the oven to 220°C/gas mark 7.

6 Sift a light dusting of flour over the top of the risen loaf. Bake in the oven for 45 minutes, or until golden brown and it sounds hollow when tapped on the bottom. If not, reduce the oven temperature to 200°C/Gas 6 and return the loaf to the oven without the tin for 5–10 minutes. Remove from the tin and cool on a wire rack.

PEANUT BUTTER SWIRL BREAD

MAKES 1 large loaf	
350ml milk, plus extra to glaze	2 tsp salt
1 tbsp maple syrup	1 tsp fast-action dried yeast
500g strong white flour, plus extra to dust	150g crunchy peanut butter
	Oil, to grease

This loaf is particularly good toasted and eaten with strawberry jam, an integrated 'PBJ'. While it is perfectly possible to make and knead this bread by hand, it is much less messy to do so by machine, owing to the stickiness of the peanut butter in the dough. You will need a 900g–1kg loaf tin.

1 Pour the milk into a small saucepan and bring to scalding point (see page 155) over a medium heat. Remove from the heat, then stir in the maple syrup and leave to cool to tepid, about 38°C.

2 Mix the flour and salt in a large bowl or the bowl of an electric food mixer and stir in the yeast. Add 100g of the peanut butter, followed by three quarters of the tepid milk. Bring the dough together with your hands, or on a low speed if using a mixer, adding more milk as necessary to make a soft dough.

3 Knead for 10 minutes by hand on the work surface (see page 12), or for 5 minutes using the dough hook of an electric mixer on low speed, until smooth and elastic.

4 Place the dough in a lightly oiled bowl and cover with lightly oiled cling film. Leave to rise for 1–2 hours, or until doubled in size. Lightly oil the loaf tin.

5 Transfer the dough to a lightly floured surface. Using a rolling pin, roll the dough out to a large rectangle, 40 x 30cm. Spread the remaining peanut butter over the middle of the dough, leaving at least a 5cm clear border around the edge.

6 Roll up the dough lengthways, like a Swiss roll. Tuck the ends underneath and fit it into the prepared loaf tin. Cover with lightly oiled cling film and leave to prove for 1 hour until increased in size by at least half, and if you press the corner lightly with your finger, it leaves only a small indentation. Meanwhile, heat the oven to 220°C/gas mark 7.

7 Brush the loaf with a little milk and bake in the top third of the oven for 20 minutes, then cover with foil, lower the oven setting to 200°C/gas mark 6 and bake for a further 20–25 minutes. It should sound hollow when removed from the tin and tapped on the bottom. If it doesn't, return it to the oven for a further 10 minutes without its tin. Cool completely on a wire rack before slicing to serve.

FIG, THYME AND HONEY BREAD

MAKES 1 small loaf

30g butter
1 tsp soft light brown sugar
150ml milk
1 tbsp tepid water
15g fresh yeast
1 small egg
125g wholemeal flour

125g strong plain white flour,
    plus extra to dust
1 tsp salt
Oil, to grease
200g dried figs
Small handful of thyme sprigs
Runny honey, to drizzle

This is the perfect bread to serve with an array of salads for a buffet lunch; the drizzled honey gives it a lovely shine. It works really well served with blue and goat's cheeses too. You will need a 450g loaf tin.

1 Use a little of the butter to grease the loaf tin, then put the remainder in a small pan with the sugar and milk. Over a medium high heat, stir to melt the sugar and butter into the milk, bring to scalding point (see page 155), then remove the pan from the heat and allow to cool to tepid.

2 Mix the tepid water with the yeast in a bowl to create a loose paste. Beat the egg, then add it to the yeast along with two thirds of the milk mixture.

3 Sift the flours and salt into a bowl. Make a well in the middle and add the yeast mixture, making sure all of the yeast is scraped out of the bowl. Mix first with a cutlery knife and then with your fingers, adding enough of the remaining milk mixture to make a soft but not sticky dough.

4 Knead the dough for 10 minutes, or until smooth and elastic (see page 12), using as little extra flour on the work surface to stop the dough sticking as possible.

5 Place the dough in a very lightly oiled bowl and cover with lightly oiled cling film or a damp tea towel and transfer to a warm place for about 1 hour to rise and double in size.

6 Slice the dried figs and set aside. Roughly chop enough thyme leaves to give you 1 tbsp.

7 Once the dough has doubled in size, remove the dough from the bowl and knead in the sliced figs and chopped thyme until well distributed. Lightly oil the loaf tin.

8 Shape the dough and place it smooth side uppermost, in the prepared loaf tin. Cover it with lightly oiled cling film and leave the loaf to prove until it is 1½ times its original size. Meanwhile, heat the oven to 200°C/gas mark 6.

9 Sift a little extra flour over the loaf and bake in the oven for 30–40 minutes, or until the loaf is golden brown, feels light for its size and sounds hollow when the bottom is tapped. Drizzle with a little honey and allow the loaf to cool on a wire rack.

APPLE CIDER BREAD

MAKES 1 large loaf	
100g dried apples	225g strong white flour,
400ml medium-dry cider	plus extra to dust
30g soft light brown sugar	225g malted brown flour
60g unsalted butter	1 tsp salt
25g fresh yeast	Oil, to grease

This is a great picnic loaf. Served with a chunk of good strong Cheddar and fruity chutney, or spread with oozing, ripe Brie and topped with thick slices of smoked ham, little else is needed except a bowl of crisp salad and a cold beer.

1 Chop the dried apples into small pieces, using kitchen scissors and put into a medium saucepan with the cider and sugar. Slowly bring to the boil over a low heat, stirring occasionally to encourage the sugar to dissolve. Lower the heat and simmer gently for 2–3 minutes.

2 Cut the butter into small pieces, add to the pan and stir for a few seconds until melted, then remove from the heat. Allow the mixture to cool, then drain over a bowl, to separate the apples from the liquid. Set aside the apple pieces for later.

3 Put the yeast in a small bowl and add 2 tbsp of the cooled liquid. Mix together until smooth and creamy.

4 Mix the flours and salt in a large bowl and make a well in the centre. Pour the yeast mixture into the well and add the remaining liquid, swilling out the yeast bowl with some of the liquid. Mix to a soft, pliable dough using a cutlery knife.

5 When the dough leaves the sides of the bowl, gather it together in your hands and, on a lightly floured surface, knead for about 10 minutes (see page 12) until smooth.

6 Put the dough in a lightly oiled bowl and cover with lightly oiled cling film. Leave in a warm place for about 1 hour until doubled in size.

7 Flatten the dough out on a lightly floured surface with the palm of your hand. Place the drained apple pieces in the centre of the dough and gather the edges to completely encase the apple. Knead to knock out the large air bubbles and to evenly distribute the fruit, about 5 minutes. You may need to use a little extra flour, as the apples are quite moist and will make the dough sticky.

8 Sift a light covering of flour over a baking sheet. Shape the dough into a tight ball and place smooth side up on the baking sheet. Flatten into a circle about 4cm thick.

9 Cover with lightly oiled cling film and leave to prove in a warm place until risen to at least half its size again, and if you press the dough lightly with your finger, it leaves only a small indentation. Meanwhile, heat the oven to 200°C/gas mark 6. About 10 minutes before it will be ready, make several deep slashes across the top of the loaf at an angle, using a very sharp knife.

10 Sift a dusting of flour over the top of the loaf and bake in the oven for 35–40 minutes until browned. Turn onto a wire rack; it should feel light and sound hollow when tapped on the underside. If not, return to the oven to cook for a further 5 minutes. Leave to cool on a wire rack.

WALNUT AND RAISIN BREAD

MAKES 1 small loaf

300ml milk
30g butter
1 tsp soft light brown sugar
10g fresh yeast
1 tbsp tepid water
125g malted brown flour

125g strong plain white flour,
   plus extra to dust
1 tsp salt
1 small egg
Oil, to grease
100g walnuts
100g raisins

Walnut and raisin is a classic flavour combination. Use this as a basic recipe to try out other fruit and nut pairings, such as pecan and cranberry, hazelnut and chopped dried apricot, or pine nut and sultana. You will need a 450–500g loaf tin.

1 Pour the milk into a small saucepan and bring to scalding point (see page 155) over a medium heat. Remove the pan from the heat.

2 Use a little of the butter to grease the loaf tin, then put the remainder in the saucepan with the hot milk and the sugar. Stir well over a medium to high heat until the sugar has dissolved and the butter has melted, then remove from the heat and leave to cool to tepid, about 38°C.

3 Put the yeast in a bowl, add the tepid water and mix to a loose paste.

4 Sift the flours and salt into a large bowl. Reserve 1 tsp of the bran from the sieve for the top of the loaf and tip the rest into the bowl with the flours.

5 Break the egg into a small bowl and beat lightly, then add it to the flours. Add the yeast mixture and three quarters of the milk and butter mixture. Mix first with a cutlery knife and then with your fingers, adding enough of the remaining milk mixture to make a soft but not sticky dough.

6 Turn out onto a very lightly floured surface and knead for about 5–8 minutes (see page 12) until smooth and elastic, using as little extra flour as possible on the work surface to stop the dough sticking.

7 Place the dough in a very lightly oiled bowl and cover with lightly oiled cling film or a damp tea towel. Leave in a warm place until doubled in size, about 1 hour.

8 Roughly chop the walnuts. Transfer the risen dough to the work surface and knock it back, kneading in the walnuts and raisins as you do so, for 2–3 minutes. Lightly oil the loaf tin.

9 Shape the dough into a loaf (see page 14) and place smooth side up in the prepared loaf tin. Cover with lightly oiled cling film and leave to prove until risen by at least half its size again. Meanwhile, heat the oven to 200°C/gas mark 6.

10 Sprinkle the reserved bran over the top of the loaf and bake in the oven for 30–40 minutes, or until golden brown and it feels light and sounds hollow when tapped on the bottom. Remove from the tin and leave to cool on a wire rack.

ROSEMARY FOCACCIA

SERVES 10–12

15g fresh yeast
275–325ml tepid water
450g strong white flour, plus
extra to dust
50g semolina
2 tsp caster sugar
10g salt, plus Maldon sea salt
for the top

30ml olive oil, plus extra
to grease and drizzle
Handful of rosemary sprigs

FOR THE TIN
2 tbsp semolina
2 tbsp olive oil

Focaccia has a characteristic uneven, open texture with large holes. It can be flavoured with various herbs, garlic or grated cheese. This focaccia, moist with olive oil, is perfect to accompany an Italian meal or al fresco lunch. You will need a 30 x 20cm shallow baking tin.

1 Put the yeast in a small bowl, add 2 tbsp of the tepid water and stir to dissolve.

2 Mix the flour, semolina, sugar and salt in a large bowl. Pour in the dissolved yeast, the oil and at least three quarters of the remaining water, using some of it to swill out any yeast stuck in the small bowl. Stir quickly, adding the remaining water if the dough feels a little dry or firm (it needs to be softer than a regular bread dough).

3 Turn the dough onto a lightly floured surface and knead until smooth and elastic (see page 12). If the dough is a little sticky, a dough scraper might be useful for this. Place in a lightly oiled bowl and cover with lightly oiled cling film. Leave in a warm place to rise until doubled in size, 1–2 hours.

4 Spread a little olive oil onto the work surface. Turn the dough out onto the oil and fold the lower third up into the middle, and the top down to cover the bottom, like a business letter. Then fold the left side into the centre, and the right side over the left. Flip the dough over so it is folded side down, then cover with the upturned bowl and leave for 20 minutes.

5 Meanwhile, mix the 2 tbsp semolina with the 2 tbsp olive oil, pour this mixture into the shallow baking tin and spread it all over the base.

6 Repeat the folding again with the dough, then place smooth side up in the baking tin. Drizzle a little olive oil over the top and spread it over the dough with your hands. Use your hands to try to encourage the dough to the edge of the baking tin, pressing rather than stretching the dough. If it feels too elastic to stretch to the edges, leave the dough to rest for 10 minutes or so, by which time it should have relaxed enough for it to spread fully to the edges.

7 Loosely cover with lightly oiled cling film and leave to rise in a warm place for 30 minutes, or until doubled in size, and if you press the corner lightly with your finger, it leaves only a small indentation. Meanwhile, heat the oven to 220°C/gas mark 7.

8 Roughly chop enough rosemary leaves to give you 2 tbsp. Sprinkle the top of the dough with the rosemary and Maldon salt, and make regular dimples by pressing your fingers into the dough firmly.

9 Transfer to the oven and bake for 15–20 minutes. You may need to turn the focaccia round halfway through cooking to ensure it becomes evenly coloured. It should be well risen, golden brown and sound hollow when tapped on the bottom. If not, return it to the oven for a few minutes. Remove from the tin to a wire rack to cool, and drizzle with a little extra olive oil.

SAGE AND GORGONZOLA FOCACCIA

SERVES 10–12	
20g fresh yeast	5 tbsp olive oil, plus extra
300–320ml tepid water	to grease and drizzle
500g strong plain flour,	150g Gorgonzola
plus extra to dust	6–8 sage leaves
2 tsp salt	½–1 tsp Maldon sea salt

With its big, gutsy flavours, this bread is a meal in itself. Serve it simply with a leafy green salad or herby tomato salad.

1 Put the yeast in a small bowl, add 4 tbsp of the water and stir to dissolve.

2 Put the flour and the 2 tsp salt into a large bowl. Pour in the yeast liquid, olive oil and at least three quarters of the remaining water, using some to swill out any yeast stuck in the small bowl. Stir quickly, adding the remaining water if the mixture feels a little dry or firm, bearing in mind that a wetter dough is better than a drier one.

3 When all the ingredients are well mixed, remove the dough to a very lightly floured surface and knead for a couple of minutes. The dough might be a little soft and wet, but don't be tempted to add more flour. A scraper is useful for this.

4 Divide the dough in half and pat or roll out with a rolling pin into 2 discs about 1.5cm thick. Place one disc on a lightly oiled baking sheet.

5 Break the Gorgonzola into small pieces and tear the sage leaves into smaller pieces. Scatter the cheese and sage on top of the dough on the baking sheet.

6 Carefully lay the second disc of dough over the filling and press the edges down to seal and encase the flavourings.

7 Cover the dough with a piece of oiled cling film and leave to rise in a warm place for about 1 hour until it has nearly doubled in size and is soft and pillowy. To check the dough has risen enough, lightly press it in one corner with your finger; it should leave a little indentation. Meanwhile, heat the oven to 200°C/ gas mark 6.

8 Remove the cling film and, using the lightly oiled fingers of one hand, make dimples at regular intervals in the dough, taking care not to push too hard and collapse the dough.

9 Drizzle with olive oil and sprinkle sparingly with Maldon sea salt (as the cheese is salty).

10 Bake in the oven for 30–40 minutes until golden. Transfer the focaccia to a wire rack and leave to cool, covering it with a tea towel to soften the crust if you wish, or leaving it uncovered if you prefer a hard crust.

ONION, RED PEPPER AND HERB BREAD

SERVES 10–12

FOR THE FILLING
1 large onion
1 garlic clove
2 tbsp olive oil
3 red peppers
Handful of thyme sprigs
Handful of basil sprigs
½ tsp caster sugar
2 tsp balsamic vinegar
Salt and freshly ground
    black pepper

FOR THE BREAD
30g fresh yeast
250ml tepid water
450g strong white flour,
    plus extra to dust
2 tsp salt
2 tbsp olive oil, plus extra
    to grease and drizzle
Thyme sprigs, to finish

To save time, this bread can also be made using jars of grilled or roasted peppers in oil, available from supermarkets. You could also crumble 85g feta into the cold filling before placing on the dough. You will need a 30 x 20cm shallow baking tin.

1 Heat the grill to its highest setting. Halve, peel and finely slice the onion and peel and crush the garlic. Heat the oil in a medium saucepan and add the sliced onions. Cover and cook over a low heat, stirring occasionally, until soft but not coloured, about 25 minutes. Add the garlic and cook for a further 2 minutes.

2 Meanwhile, cut the peppers into quarters and remove the seeds, then arrange, skin side up, over a large baking sheet that will fit under the grill. Grill the peppers, in batches if necessary, until the skins are black and blistered. Put them in a bowl, cover tightly with cling film and leave to steam for 10 minutes, to loosen their skins. Chop enough thyme and basil leaves to give you 2 tbsp of each.

3 Skin the peppers and cut them into thick slices. Add them with the sugar to the onions, increase the heat and allow the peppers and onions to caramelise a little. Add the vinegar and chopped herbs. Boil off any liquid, then season to taste with salt and pepper and set aside to cool.

4 Meanwhile, to make the dough, dissolve the yeast in the tepid water. Sift the flour and salt into a large bowl and make a well in the centre. Pour in the dissolved yeast and the oil. Quickly mix the ingredients to form a dough, then knead the dough on a lightly floured surface for 10 minutes (see page 12).

5 Put the dough in a lightly oiled bowl, cover with oiled cling film and leave in a warm place to rise for 1 hour, or until doubled in size. Oil the baking tin.

6 Tip the risen dough out onto a lightly floured surface and cut it in half. Roll out one half, using a rolling pin, to a rectangle the size and shape of the baking tin. Ease it into the tin and stretch it a little, if necessary, to cover the base. Cover with the pepper and onion mixture and roll the other piece of dough out to the same size. Carefully lay it on top, excluding as much air as possible. Press down and seal the edges with a little water, using a pastry brush. Cover with lightly oiled cling film and leave to prove for 15 minutes. Meanwhile, heat the oven to 200°C/gas mark 6.

7 When the dough feels soft and pillowy, make indentations over the surface with your fingers. Drizzle oil into the holes and insert thyme sprigs. Bake in the oven for 30–40 minutes until it sounds hollow when tapped on the underside. Carefully lift the loaf onto a wire rack to cool. Cut into squares to serve.

MEDITERRANEAN PARMESAN TEARING BREAD

30g fresh yeast
Pinch of caster sugar
300ml tepid water
450g strong white flour,
 plus extra to dust
2 tsp salt

1 tbsp olive oil, plus extra
 to drizzle
50g Parmesan cheese
Bunch of basil
85g sun-dried tomatoes in oil

This bread is made with a large quantity of yeast and so is quite quick to make. It has a craggy, rocky finish. Place it in the middle of the table on a board and allow everyone to help themselves by pulling off pieces. It is highly flavoured and so perfect for serving with an otherwise simple salad meal.

1 Put the yeast and sugar in a small bowl and stir in enough of the tepid water to make a smooth liquid.

2 Mix the flour and salt in a large bowl and make a well in the centre. Add the dissolved yeast, swilling out the yeast bowl with a little more of the water to ensure none is lost. Add three quarters of the remaining water and the olive oil. Gradually draw in the flour and bring the mixture together into a soft dough, adding the remaining liquid if needed.

3 Knead the dough for 8–10 minutes (see page 12) until smooth and elastic. Put the dough into a lightly oiled bowl and cover with lightly oiled cling film. Leave to rise in a warm place until doubled in size and soft and pillowy to the touch, about 30 minutes. Dust a large baking sheet with flour.

4 Grate the Parmesan, roughly chop the basil and slice the sun-dried tomatoes. Scatter all of these ingredients over a large board and cover with the dough (as shown). Using your largest chopping knife, chop the dough into pieces (as shown). Now push the pieces back together. Repeat this twice more, until the cheese, tomato and basil are evenly distributed in seams through the dough.

5 Push the pieces of dough into a rough circle and transfer it to the floured baking sheet (it doesn't matter if it is not fully stuck together as the loaf will continue to form as it proves and bakes).

6 Cover the dough loosely with lightly oiled cling film and leave for 20–30 minutes, or until it has increased in size by half again, and if you press the corner lightly with your finger, it leaves only a small indentation. Meanwhile, heat the oven to 200°C/gas mark 6.

7 Drizzle olive oil over the surface of the dough, then bake in the oven until brown and it sounds hollow when tapped on the underside, 30–40 minutes. Transfer to a wire rack to cool.

GLUTEN-FREE BREADS

Gluten is found in varying quantities in many different flours, including spelt, oats, barley and rye, although all of these are relatively low in gluten and can be eaten by those who have only a mild gluten intolerance.

There are now many varieties of mixed gluten-free flours on the market. We use Doves Farm at the time of writing, which is a mixture of rice, potato, tapioca, maize and buckwheat flours.

Without gluten, textures tend to be rather crumbly when baked, so xanthan gum (made from corn sugar) or gelatine is often added to lend adhesive and elastic properties in place of gluten.

If you would like to try adapting other recipes in this book to being gluten-free, use a good-quality gluten-free flour and add 1 tsp xanthan gum for each 250g gluten-free flour you use. The gluten-free flour will also need more water than wheat flour.

POPPY SEED GLUTEN-FREE BREAD

MAKES 1 small loaf

20ml rapeseed oil, plus
　　extra to oil
235g strong plain gluten-free
　　flour (we use Doves Farm),
　　plus extra to dust
½ tsp salt, plus a pinch
25g caster sugar

1¼ tsp xanthan gum
½ tbsp poppy seeds
1 tsp powdered gelatine
½ tbsp fast-action dried yeast
1 egg, plus 1 egg white
200ml tepid water

Here poppy seeds are used to add texture to a gluten-free loaf but you could substitute other seeds, such as sesame, sunflower or pumpkin seeds, or even chopped nuts if you like. You will need a 450–500g loaf tin.

1 Lightly brush the loaf tin with oil.

2 Put the flour, salt, sugar, xanthan gum, poppy seeds, gelatine and yeast into a large bowl and mix thoroughly using a whisk.

3 In a separate bowl, beat the whole egg and egg white together with a fork to break them up.

4 Add about three quarters of the water, along with the oil and beaten egg, to the dry ingredients. Mix vigorously with a wooden spoon, or using the 'k' beater of a food mixer on

a slow speed for 2–3 minutes until the mixture is smooth and a reluctant dropping consistency, adding more water if necessary. The mixture should have the consistency of a Victoria sponge cake mixture. Scrape the mixture into the prepared tin and leave to rise in a warm place for about 35 minutes, or until doubled in size. Meanwhile, heat the oven to 200°C/gas mark 6.

5 Sift a little flour over the loaf and bake in the top third of the oven for 40–50 minutes, or until the loaf sounds hollow when tapped on the bottom. After the first 10 minutes, you may need to place some foil over the top of the loaf to prevent it from colouring too much.

6 Remove the loaf from the tin and allow to cool completely on a wire rack.

GLUTEN-FREE FOCACCIA

SERVES 6–8

110g strong plain gluten-free
   flour (we use Doves Farm)
220g cornflour
55g ground almonds
2 tsp salt
2 tsp xanthan gum
2 tsp caster sugar

14g fast-action dried yeast
350ml tepid water
2 tbsp olive oil, plus extra
   to grease and drizzle
1 lemon
Few rosemary sprigs
1 tsp Maldon sea salt

This is a really versatile gluten-free bread recipe given to us by Adriana Rabinovich who teaches gluten-free baking classes here at Leiths. This dough can also be used to make pizza bases and Swedish style cracker bread. It has the added virtue of being dairy- and egg-free in addition to containing no wheat or gluten.

1 Mix the flour, cornflour, ground almonds, salt, xanthan gum, sugar and yeast in a large bowl. Stir well with a whisk until the ingredients are well mixed.

2 In a measuring jug, combine the tepid water and oil, then add to the dry ingredients,, mixing with a wooden spoon. The dough will come together and should be soft and a little wet. If it seems dry, add a little more water but don't overdo it. Beat with a wooden spoon for about 1 minute until it comes away from the sides of the bowl. Don't be alarmed that the dough is very sloppy!

3 Turn the dough out onto a sheet of silicone paper or baking parchment. Dip both hands in cold water and gently flatten the dough into an oblong shape of an even thickness, about 3cm.

4 Cover loosely with lightly oiled cling film and leave to rise for 15–20 minutes. Meanwhile, heat the oven to 220°C/gas mark 7 and put a baking tray upside down in the oven to heat up.

5 Dip your fingers in cold water and make indentations into the dough at regular intervals. Cover with lightly oiled cling film again and leave to rise for a further 5 minutes. Finely grate enough lemon zest to give about ½ tsp and finely chop enough rosemary to give you 2 tsp.

6 Sprinkle the lemon zest over the loaf, drizzle with some olive oil and scatter over the rosemary and sea salt. Lift the dough on its paper onto a flat tray to transport to the oven. Slide the focaccia still on its paper directly onto the hot tray in the oven and bake in the oven for 20–25 minutes until golden brown.

7 To test if the bread is fully cooked, gently tap the underside with your knuckles; it should sound hollow. If not, bake for a few more minutes. Lift the focaccia, still on its paper, onto a wire rack to cool slightly for a few minutes before cutting into squares or tearing into chunks to serve.

To make pizza...

✱ Divide the dough into three, spread each piece thinly on a piece of baking parchment and leave to rise for 15–20 minutes. Just before placing in the oven, drizzle with a little olive oil. Lift the dough, still on the paper directly onto a heated tray in the oven as above. Bake for 8–10 minutes. Remove from the oven and place your chosen toppings on the baked crust. Return to the oven to bake until the toppings are melted and golden.

2

SOURDOUGHS

Artisan breads from all over the world are made using varying types of starter doughs. These doughs have different names – bigas, poolish and levains to name a few – and they are prepared with different quantities of ingredients according to their country or region of origin, but the principle remains the same.

Breads made using a starter dough have a characteristic chewy texture, thick crust and slightly sour, complex flavour, hence the name 'sourdough'. They also have better keeping qualities than loaves made using just yeast. The classic sourdough loaf is made with a starter that uses natural wild yeasts. Also included here are loaves made from a starter that uses commercial yeast, namely rye bread and ciabatta.

STARTER DOUGHS

Some starter doughs are made using commercial yeast, and some using only the naturally occurring yeasts present in the air around us. Using commercial yeast makes the result more predictable and we think this is the best place to start when making these sourdough type loaves for the first time. Using natural yeasts is a project in which you will need to invest some time, and learn as you go. The starter dough you make can be nurtured and kept alive for years!

MAKING A STARTER DOUGH WITH COMMERCIAL YEAST

When making a starter dough with commercial yeast, roughly half the yeast used to rise a loaf of bread is mixed with some of the flour to make a batter, sometimes with sweetening ingredients such as sugar or honey, but never with salt which slows down the yeast. This starter is stirred and then allowed to ferment, at least overnight. The remaining ingredients are then added and the bread is mixed, kneaded and risen as usual.

You can experiment with all the yeasted recipes in this and any book, by adapting them and making a starter dough with some of their ingredients.

MAKING SOURDOUGH FROM A WILD YEAST STARTER

We are not going to pretend that making sourdough is always easy to master. The speed with which the starter matures can vary and you will need to spend some time getting to know your starter, so there may be a few mistakes along the way. However, it is one of the most rewarding and satisfying things to cook – well worth a little trouble.

We use organic flour here as we want to do everything possible to encourage the wild yeasts to flourish in the starter dough. Rye flour seems to result in a more lively starter dough and so we use some along with the higher gluten white flour in order to be able to use the starter to make bread after only a week of development. Some natural starters made without rye may take several weeks to be ready. (Once you have mastered the basic method, do try this; the flavour is more highly developed as the starter has matured for longer.)

It is possible to make a wild yeast starter dough in the middle of a city as we have done often, but it is easier in the countryside where the air naturally contains a better mixture of yeasts.

Tips for making and using a wild yeast starter...

✳ If ever in doubt about whether your starter is ready to bake with, do the float test.

✳ Use the starter when it is active and hungry, rather than when it has just been fed. So, take out the quantity you need and then feed the remainder.

✳ If the starter has been in the fridge for a long time, a liquid may form on the top. Just pour it off before using the starter.

✳ If the starter has been in the fridge for a long time, when you take it out, transfer it to a large bowl to allow a greater surface area to come into contact with the air.

SETTING UP A WILD YEAST SOURDOUGH STARTER

1 Weigh a heavy glass Kilner jar, and write the weight on it. (This helps when you need to work out how much of the starter to discard later in the week.) Weigh 25g organic strong white flour and 25g organic rye flour into the jar, add 50ml water (at room temperature) and stir until it forms a rough dough. It doesn't have to be completely smooth, but try to make sure there are no dry patches. Leave this mixture, uncovered, in a draught-free place for 24 hours.

2 At the same time the following day, discard half the initial starter from the jar so you are left with 50g. Add 25g each of white and rye flour with 50ml water to the remaining mixture, and stir well. As before, leave uncovered for 24 hours.

3 Repeat this process over a total of 5 days, still with the jar uncovered. By this time, there should be a bit of activity in the jar – bubbles are an indication that the yeast is developing. If you can see some sign that the starter has risen and fallen during the day and has small bubbles dispersed throughout, you can feed it for a second time on day 6 after discarding half of the mixture as before. Otherwise, just feed it once.

4 On day 7, feed it twice. If possible, try to feed it a little earlier in the day the first time to allow it time to bubble before feeding again. You should see a honeycomb network of bubbles underneath the surface.

5 Keep feeding your starter twice a day until it is ready to use, discarding half the mixture as before. It is ready to use when it passes the 'float test', below.

THE FLOAT TEST

To test when a starter dough is ready to use, drop a spoonful into a bowl of cold water. It should be bubbly and airy enough to float.

LOOKING AFTER YOUR STARTER

If you are going to be baking regularly, you can keep the starter out, uncovered, at room temperature, and keep feeding it twice a day. To feed, you need to double its weight each time. So if it weighs 200g, you would add 100g flour and 100ml water. Obviously, if you continue doing this, you will end up with a ridiculous amount of starter, so you either have to bake with it or throw some away. Once the starter has reached this stage, there is no need to keep mixing the white flour with rye flour for feeding; you can just use white flour.

However, if you are not baking daily, the starter doesn't need constant looking after, so if you want to go on holiday, there's no need to take it with you! To keep it dormant in the fridge, feed it, and put it in a large jar, ideally a Kilner jar with the rubber seal removed so some gas can escape, and just make sure it's only about one third full (much fuller than that and the last feed will make it bubble up and overflow in the fridge).

Two days before you're ready to bake, take the starter from the fridge, remove the lid and put the starter into a medium bowl. Double its weight by feeding with flour as before, twice a day until it passes the float test. If it has been in the fridge for quite a long time, it may take a little longer to be ready to bake, but if you're baking fairly frequently, 2 days should be sufficient.

SOURDOUGH LOAF

MAKES 1 large round loaf

100g sourdough starter, out of the fridge for 2 days (see page 55)
375ml tepid water

500g strong white flour, plus extra to dust
12g salt
Oil, to grease

If you have a baking stone, put it on the oven shelf when you heat the oven and use it in place of the floured baking sheet. Be careful when you remove it and invert the dough onto it, as it will be very hot.

1 Put the starter into a large bowl and mix in 350ml of the water. Whisk thoroughly with a balloon whisk. Add the flour all at once, then mix it quickly together to form a fairly scrappy and softish dough; a plastic dough scraper is particularly useful for this. Add a little extra water if necessary. At this stage, it does not matter too much how smooth the dough is, just make sure there are no dry patches of flour. Leave the dough to rest for about 30 minutes. This helps the flour to absorb all the liquid and will make kneading easier.

2 Mix the salt with the remaining 25ml water and add this to the dough. Mix it in by bringing the sides of the dough into the middle. Keep turning the bowl, folding the sides of the dough into the middle each time, until it is mixed; this will take about 30 seconds. Leave the dough to rest again for 10 minutes.

3 Fold the dough in the bowl again. If you find that the dough is sticking to your hand, dampen your hand a little. Leave to rest for another 10 minutes.

4 Repeat the folding and resting cycle about 8 times in total. It might seem like a lot of work, but each fold only takes about 30 seconds, if not less, so the actual contact time with the dough is minimal. After the final folds, the dough should be noticeably smoother and elastic.

5 Place the dough in a lightly oiled bowl, cover with lightly oiled cling film and leave to rise until doubled in size, either about 2 hours at room temperature, or overnight in the fridge.

6 Very lightly flour the work surface. Using a dough scraper or your hands, turn the dough out onto the flour, trying not to knock too many air bubbles out as the texture and crumb structure of sourdough is usually more open and airy than normal bread.

7 Gently shape the dough into a rough rectangle. Fold the top of the dough down to the middle, and the bottom over it, a little like a business letter. Then fold the left side in, and the right side over it. Flip the loaf over, so that all the folds are underneath, lightly cover with oiled cling film and leave to rest for about 20 minutes. Then turn the dough smooth side down again onto a lightly floured surface and repeat the folding process once again. Flip again so the folds are underneath.

8 Generously flour a proving basket, or a deep bowl lined with a clean tea towel. Put the dough in, smooth side down, cover with oiled cling film and leave to prove until doubled in size and a finger inserted in a corner leaves an indentation. Sourdoughs often take a long time to prove, as natural yeasts are not as powerful as commercially produced yeast, and it is often very tempting to get the dough into the oven before it is sufficiently proved. It may take up to 4 hours at room temperature, or overnight in the fridge. Feel the top of the dough with the flat of your hand; it should feel spongy and airy.

9 At least 30 minutes before you bake your loaf, heat the oven to 225°C/gas mark 8. Position the oven shelf towards the top third of the oven, bearing in mind that the bread will rise and it will stick to the roof of the oven if too high up. Place a roasting tin in the bottom of the oven and lightly flour a baking sheet.

10 When the dough is ready to bake, pour 500ml boiling water into the roasting tin in the oven. Very carefully remove the cling film and invert the dough onto the baking sheet. Immediately, using a very sharp knife, score a pattern on the top of the bread. This encourages it to rise evenly, and also creates some really good crunchy crust.

STEP 2 Repeatedly folding the sides of the dough into the middle to mix it thoroughly, turning the bowl with the other hand to ensure the dough is evenly worked.

STEP 4 Folding the dough for the final time; at this stage it is smooth and elastic.

STEP 6 Carefully turning the risen dough out of the bowl onto a floured surface to avoid knocking out too many air bubbles, using a dough scraper.

STEP 7 Folding the dough: bringing the left side of the dough to the middle and the right side over it.

(Continued overleaf)

STEP 8 Testing the proving dough, once it has doubled in size, by inserting a finger in the corner. If it leaves an indentation the dough is ready to bake.

STEP 10 Scoring the top of the loaf before baking with a sharp knife, to encourage even rising and the formation of a good crust.

11 Open the oven door carefully, protecting your hands and forearms from the steam. Slide the baking sheet onto the positioned shelf, close the door and bake for 25–30 minutes. After 15 minutes, turn the bread around so that it colours evenly. When cooked it will be risen, deep brown and, if you tap it on the base, it should sound hollow. It will feel heavier than a normal bread; this is fine. If it needs a little more baking, turn the oven down to 180°C/gas mark 4 until cooked.

12 Allow to cool completely on a wire rack.

A note on folding and turning...

✳ Folding and turning the dough gently rather than kneading helps to build and strengthen gluten gently, bringing the gluten strands into alignment. In addition, it gets rid of any excess carbon dioxide, which would otherwise inhibit the less vigorous wild yeast. When making sourdough, the yeast moves more slowly, so it makes sense to allow the bread to take its time. With a bread raised with commercial yeast, the yeast moves so quickly that it would have fully risen by the end of the folding and turning process.

A note on resting dough...

✳ By allowing the just-mixed dough to rest as described in step 1, it will have already absorbed the liquid and even started developing a bit of gluten by the time you come to knead, so the kneading process will be much quicker and easier.

A note on adding salt later...

✳ While salt is essential to both the taste and structure of bread, it can be useful to omit it while the less powerful wild yeast starts to work. Salt inhibits the growth of the yeast as well as the ability of the flour to absorb liquid, and some time without it at the beginning of the process speeds up the mixing and kneading. You will find that the dough, without salt, is much smoother and much easier to deal with.

DARK RYE BREAD

MAKES 2 small loaves

FOR THE STARTER
10g fresh yeast
170ml tepid water
70g rye flour
70g strong white flour
15g whole or ground linseeds
50g sunflower seeds
1 tbsp molasses

FOR THE DOUGH
15g fresh yeast
150–200ml tepid water
300g rye flour, plus extra
  to dust
100g spelt flour
1½–2 tsp salt
1 tbsp runny honey
Oil, to grease
1 tbsp milk, to brush
Extra seeds, to sprinkle

This bread has a lovely deep flavour, making it the perfect partner for strong, punchy flavours, such as cured meats and pickles, or for balancing smooth and mellow soft cheeses. It needs to be started a day in advance. You can use any small seeds in place of linseeds. You will need two 450–500g loaf tins.

1 To make the starter, put the yeast and 2–3 tbsp of the tepid water in a small bowl and stir until dissolved. Mix the flours in a large bowl, and add the seeds and molasses. Add the yeast, swilling out the yeast bowl with the remaining water to ensure none is lost, and stir in well. Cover the bowl with cling film and leave it in a cool place overnight. If it is very warm, put the starter in the fridge overnight, but you will need to bring it up to room temperature again before using it.

2 The next day, to make the dough, put the yeast in a small bowl, add 2 tbsp of the tepid water and stir to dissolve. Mix the flours and salt in a large bowl. Make a well in the centre and tip the starter into the well, along with the new yeast mixture and the honey.

3 Add three quarters of the remaining water (using some of it to swill out the yeast bowl). Use a cutlery knife to distribute the liquid evenly through the flour mix and bring the mixture together into a dough, adding more water if required to make a soft but not sticky dough.

4 Transfer the dough to a very lightly floured surface and knead for 10–12 minutes (see page 12) until smooth and elastic. Put the dough in a lightly oiled bowl, cover with lightly oiled cling film and leave to rise in a warm place until doubled in size, about 1 hour.

5 Transfer the dough to the work surface and knock it back, kneading it for 2–3 minutes. Lightly oil the loaf tin.

6 Divide the dough in half, shape into 2 loaves (see page 14) and place them in the oiled tins. Cover with lightly oiled cling film and leave in a warm, but not too hot, place to prove, for about 1 hour. To check the dough is proved enough, lightly press it in one corner with your finger; it should leave only a little indentation. Meanwhile, heat the oven to 200°C/gas mark 6.

7 Lightly brush the tops of the loaves with milk and sprinkle with a few seeds. Bake in the oven for 25–35 minutes until browned. The loaves should also feel light for their size and sound hollow when tapped on the underside. If not, return them to the oven for a few minutes.

8 Leave to cool in the tins for 10 minutes before removing and turning out onto a wire rack to cool.

CIABATTA

MAKES 1 large loaf

FOR THE STARTER
7g fresh yeast
175ml water (at room
    temperature)
125g strong white flour

FOR THE DOUGH
1 tbsp olive oil, plus extra
    to grease
1 tsp salt
125g strong white flour,
    plus extra to dust
1 tbsp fine polenta

Start this dough a day in advance, to allow the flavours time to develop, and you will appreciate a much more complex flavour than most bought ciabattas offer. You might like to knead in chopped olives, torn basil leaves or chopped thyme to add flavour to the basic dough, although a plain ciabatta is delicious. Unlike many loaves that use a starter dough, this recipe does not require more yeast in addition to the starter dough. You will need a 900g–1kg loaf tin for proving.

1 To make the starter dough, put the yeast into a large bowl and stir in the water followed by the flour. Cover the bowl with cling film and leave to stand in a cool place for at least 1–2 hours, but ideally overnight.

2 The following day (or at least 2 hours later), stir the olive oil, salt and flour into the starter dough. Bring the dough together, turn it out onto the work surface and knead (see page 12) for 10 minutes. The dough will be sticky but try not to add too much flour while you knead; a pastry scraper is useful when kneading a sticky dough like this. Lightly oil the loaf tin.

3 When the dough is smooth and elastic, gather it back into a ball and place in the oiled loaf tin. Cover with lightly oiled cling film and leave to rise in a cool place until doubled in size, about 1–2 hours, and if you press the corner lightly with your finger, it leaves only a small indentation.

4 Meanwhile, heat the oven to 220°C/gas mark 7, place a roasting tin on the bottom shelf of the oven and fill it with boiling water from the kettle. This will provide steam to give the loaf its characteristic crust.

5 Scatter the polenta and plenty of flour over a baking sheet. Carefully turn the loaf tin upside down onto the prepared baking sheet and let the dough gently come away from the sides of the tin. With floured hands, gently coax it into an long oval shape, handling the dough carefully to avoid knocking out any air. Dust the surface of the loaf with flour.

6 Bake in the top third of the oven for 25–30 minutes, or until light golden. When cooked, the loaf should feel very light for its size and sound hollow when tapped on the underside. Cool the loaf on a wire rack before serving.

3

ROLLS, FLAT BREADS AND BREADSTICKS

This chapter showcases delicious rolls and breads from around the world, as well as providing lots of ideas for shaping and flavouring more traditional doughs. There is nothing quite like a batch of freshly baked rolls to accompany a meal when you are entertaining. Try the fresh herb naan breads (on page 78) alongside a spiced soup or curry, or taralli pugliesi (on page 76) with an antipasti of Italian cured meats, salami and salads.

Many of the bread dough recipes featured earlier in this book as large loaves can also be made into bread rolls. Just weigh them to ensure all the rolls will be the same size and reduce the cooking time accordingly.

ENRICHED BREAD ROLLS

MAKES about 24 rolls (or 18 larger baps)

300–350ml milk	500g strong plain flour,
30g butter	plus extra to dust
20g fresh yeast	2 tsp salt
1 tsp caster sugar	2 eggs
	Oil, to grease

1 Put the milk in a small saucepan and bring to scalding point (see page 155) over a medium heat. Remove from the heat, transfer 2 tbsp to a small bowl and set aside to cool to tepid, about 38°C. Cut the butter into small dice and add to the remaining milk in the pan. Leave to melt and cool to tepid.

2 Add the yeast and sugar to the cooled milk in the bowl and stir until dissolved.

3 Put the flour and salt into a large bowl.

4 Lightly beat 1 egg in a bowl, then add to the flour along with the dissolved yeast and at least three quarters of the milk and butter mixture (use some of it to swill out any remaining yeast in its bowl). Use a cutlery knife to distribute the liquid evenly and bring the ingredients together into a dough. Add more milk and butter if necessary to create a soft, slightly tacky dough.

5 When the dough is starting to form, use your hands to bring it together. Transfer to a very lightly floured surface and knead for 5–8 minutes (see page 12) until smooth and elastic.

6 Put the dough into a large, very lightly oiled bowl, cover with lightly oiled cling film and leave to rise in a warm place until doubled in size, about 1 hour.

7 Transfer the risen dough to the work surface and knock it back, kneading it for 2–3 minutes.

8 Divide the dough into equal-sized pieces, each 35–45g, or 50–55g for baps. Shape into rolls (see right) and place on a lightly greased large baking sheet. Cover loosely with lightly oiled cling film and leave the rolls to prove in a warm place for 10–15 minutes. Meanwhile, heat the oven to 200°C/gas mark 6. Beat the other egg with a fork, then sieve it.

9 To check the dough has proved enough, lightly press it in one corner with your finger; it should leave only a little indentation. Brush the rolls with beaten egg and bake in the top third of the oven for 10–15 minutes until golden.

10 Transfer the rolls to a wire rack; they should feel light and sound hollow when tapped on the underside. If not, return to the oven for a further 3–5 minutes. Leave to cool on a wire rack; for softer rolls, keep covered with a tea towel as they cool.

Variations

✱ **Crown** Shape as for plain rolls and cut a cross in the top before proving (illustrated overleaf).

✱ **Pawnbroker** Divide the small ball of dough into 3 equal pieces. Form each piece into a ball and place next to each other on the baking sheet to make a triangle (illustrated overleaf).

✱ **Catherine wheel** Shape the small ball of dough into a sausage about 15cm long. Coil the dough round from the centre, forming a catherine wheel (illustrated overleaf).

✱ **Knot** Shape the small ball of dough into a sausage about 15cm long. Carefully, without stretching, tie the dough into a knot. Try to hide the ends under the knot (illustrated overleaf).

✱ **Pointed** Carefully roll opposite ends of the small ball between your hand and the table into tapered points. The points of dough can be gently twisted (illustrated overleaf).

✱ **Baps** Shape as for plain rolls, but flatten the tops even more.

TECHNIQUE
SHAPING PLAIN ROLLS

It is worth being a little more precise when shaping rolls, as the aim is to make each roll in a batch look uniform. We would advise you to weigh the dough and calculate the exact weight each roll should be to ensure they will all be the same size. Rolls can be spaced out on the baking sheet with room between them to ensure they don't join together when proving or baking, or they can be spaced so that they will join at the edges; this is called batch baking.

Fresh cooled rolls can be successfully frozen in a sealed plastic bag and defrosted for use. Place the defrosted rolls in the oven, preheated to 190°C/gas mark 5, for 3 minutes to crisp them up before serving.

1 Divide the knocked back dough into equal pieces and shape into balls. Take a ball and gently stretch and pull the dough towards the top, creating a smooth surface underneath.

2 Turn the roll over so the smooth side is uppermost, and neaten the roll with the sides of your hands. Shape the other rolls, working quickly to ensure the first ones do not over-prove.

3 Place the rolls on a lightly greased baking sheet, spacing them apart. Lightly pat down the tops to flatten a little.

SHAPING A PAWNBROKER
Place 3 equal-sized small balls of dough together to form a trefoil-shaped roll.

SHAPING A CATHERINE WHEEL
Coil the sausage of dough to form a spiral.

SHAPING A KNOT
Tie the sausage of dough into a knot and hide the ends underneath.

SHAPING A POINTED ROLL
Roll the opposite ends of the ball of dough to flatten and taper into points.

SOFT WHITE HERBY ROLLS

MAKES 12–15	
300ml milk	20g fresh yeast
450g strong white flour, plus extra to dust	1 tsp caster sugar
	1 egg
50g cornflour	Oil, to grease
Scant 2 tsp salt	Few soft herb sprigs, such as
30g butter	basil, parsley or coriander

An excellent accompaniment to soups, these are also ideal picnic sandwich baps. For a pronounced herby flavour you will need at least 4 tbsp of chopped herbs; use less if you prefer a more subtle taste.

1 Pour the milk into a small saucepan and bring to scalding point (see page 155) over a medium heat, then remove from the heat and cool to tepid, about 38°C.

2 Sift the flour, cornflour and salt into a large bowl. Cut the butter into small pieces and rub it into the flour using your fingertips. In a small bowl, dissolve the yeast with a little of the tepid milk and the sugar.

3 Break the egg into a small bowl and beat using a fork to break it up. Pour into the flour with the yeast mixture. Swill the yeast bowl out with milk to make sure it all goes into the dough and then add enough of the remaining milk to make a soft but not sticky dough.

4 Knead the dough for 5–8 minutes (see page 12) until elastic and smooth. Put into a lightly oiled bowl and cover with lightly oiled cling film. Leave to rise in a warm place until doubled in size, about 1 hour.

5 When risen, knock the dough back for a few minutes and tear some herbs over it, about 4 tbsp. Knead just to distribute the herbs through the dough, then divide the dough into 12–15 even pieces and shape each into a flattish oval.

6 Place on 2 lightly floured baking sheets, cover with lightly oiled cling film and leave to prove until nearly doubled in size, and if you lightly press a roll with your finger, it leaves only a small indentation. Meanwhile, heat the oven to 200°C/gas mark 6.

7 Sift a little flour over the rolls and bake in the oven for 20 minutes, or until light golden and they feel light for their size. Remove from the oven, transfer to a wire rack and cover with a clean tea towel to soften their crust as they cool.

SEMOLINA AND PARMESAN ROLLS

MAKES 20–22

FOR THE STARTER
5g fresh yeast
90ml tepid water
¼ tsp caster sugar
70g strong white flour

FOR THE DOUGH
15g fresh yeast
300–350ml tepid water
300g strong white flour,
    plus extra to dust
200g semolina
2 tsp salt
Oil, to grease
120g Parmesan cheese

These dinner rolls are made using a starter dough, which needs to be left in the fridge overnight. This allows the flavour to develop, which along with the Parmesan gives really tangy and delicious results. To read more about starter doughs, see page 54.

1 To make the starter, put the yeast in a bowl, add the water and stir to dissolve the yeast. Add the sugar and flour and stir to combine, then cover the bowl with cling film and leave in the fridge overnight.

2 The next day, for the dough, combine the yeast with 2 tbsp of the water in a small bowl and stir well. Sift the flour and semolina into a large bowl and add the salt. Make a well in the centre of the flour and add the starter dough as well as the dissolved yeast. Add three quarters of the remaining water, using some of it to swill out the yeast bowl. Stir the mixture quickly to bring it together into a soft but not sticky dough.

3 Turn the dough out onto a lightly floured surface and knead for 8–10 minutes (see page 12) until smooth and elastic, using as little extra flour as possible on the work surface to stop the dough from sticking. Place in a very lightly oiled bowl and cover with lightly oiled cling film. Leave in a warm place until doubled in size, about 1 hour. Grate the Parmesan and set aside.

4 Transfer the risen dough to the work surface and knock it back for a couple of minutes. Press the dough out into a disc, then place 100g of the grated Parmesan in the centre of the disc, pull the edges over to enclose completely, and knead until the Parmesan is thoroughly incorporated.

5 Shape the dough into rolls (see page 67), each 35–45g, and transfer them to a lightly oiled baking sheet. It helps to work quickly as the rolls that are shaped first will begin to rise again as soon as they are shaped. Cover with lightly oiled cling film and leave to prove in a warm place for about 1 hour. Meanwhile, heat the oven to 200°C/gas mark 6.

6 To check the dough is proved enough, lightly press a roll at the bottom near the baking sheet with your finger; it should leave only a little indentation.

7 Sprinkle a little of the remaining Parmesan over the top of each roll and bake in the oven for 15–20 minutes until lightly golden. The rolls should sound hollow when tapped on the base. Remove them to a wire rack to cool.

SWEET POTATO AND PUMPKIN SEED ROLLS

MAKES 12	
200ml milk	10g fast-action dried yeast
200g sweet potato	2 tbsp olive oil, plus extra
450g strong white flour	to grease
2 tsp salt	1 tsp runny honey
40g pumpkin seeds,	2 tbsp lemon juice
plus extra to sprinkle	1 egg

These require less kneading than other yeasted bread rolls so they are quick to make. If possible, use a bright orange variety of sweet potato, as it will give the rolls a fantastic vibrant colour.

1 Pour the milk into a small saucepan and bring to scalding point (see page 155) over a medium heat, then remove from the heat and cool to tepid, about 38°C. Peel and finely grate the sweet potato; you should have about 180g.

2 Mix the flour and salt in a large bowl and stir in the pumpkin seeds, grated sweet potato and yeast. Stir in the oil, honey, lemon juice and enough of the tepid milk to make a soft but not sticky dough.

3 Tip out onto a lightly floured surface and knead the dough for 2–3 minutes (see page 12) until just elastic. Put it into a lightly oiled bowl, cover with lightly oiled cling film and leave to rise for 30–40 minutes, or until doubled in size.

4 Divide the dough into 12 equal pieces and shape into balls (see page 67). The dough can be sticky, so lightly flour your hands, if necessary, while you shape them. Flatten each ball slightly with the palm of your hand as you arrange them on 2 lightly oiled baking sheets. Cover with lightly oiled cling film and leave in a warm place for 20 minutes to prove until increased in size by half, and if you press the dough lightly with your finger, it leaves only a small indentation. Meanwhile, heat the oven to 200°C/gas mark 6.

5 Beat the egg in a small bowl using a fork, then sieve it. Lightly brush the tops of the rolls with the egg, then sprinkle with a few pumpkin seeds.

6 Bake in the oven for 10 minutes, then swap the baking sheets around in the oven and bake for a further 5 minutes. Lower the oven setting to 190°C/gas mark 5 and continue to cook until the rolls sound hollow when tapped on the bottom. Transfer to a wire rack to cool.

LEEK AND CHEDDAR ROLLS

MAKES 10	
300ml milk, plus extra to glaze	60g butter
20g fresh yeast	2 tbsp wholegrain mustard
1 tsp caster sugar	1 tbsp oil, plus extra to grease
250g wholemeal flour	3 leeks
250g strong white flour, plus extra to dust	150g Cheddar cheese
2 tsp salt	1 egg

These buns are almost a meal in themselves, with their cheesy top and savoury leek and mustard flavour. They would also work well accompanying a vegetable soup or filled with ham and pickles for picnics.

1 Bring the milk to scalding point (see page 155) in a small pan, then allow it to cool to tepid, about 38°C.

2 In a small bowl, dissolve the yeast in 2–3 tbsp of the tepid milk, then stir in the sugar.

3 Sift the flours and salt into a large bowl, tipping in any bran left in the sieve. Cut the butter into small dice and add it to the flour, then rub it in with your fingertips. Make a well in the centre of the flour and add the yeast mixture, mustard and the remaining tepid milk. Bring the dough together using a cutlery knife, adding a little extra milk or water if needed to make a soft dough.

4 Transfer the dough to a lightly floured surface and knead for 5–8 minutes (see page 12) until smooth and elastic. Return the dough to the lightly oiled bowl and cover the bowl with lightly oiled cling film. Leave to rise in a warm place for about 1 hour until doubled in size.

5 Meanwhile, finely chop the leeks and wash thoroughly in a sieve to remove any grit. Heat the oil in a small pan, add the leeks and cook over a gentle heat until softened, without browning. Remove the leeks from the pan and set aside to cool.

6 Once the leeks have cooled, place them in a sieve and press down firmly with the back of a wooden spoon to drain away any liquid. Oil a large baking sheet and grate the cheese.

7 Transfer the dough back to the work surface and flatten it out with your hands, then sprinkle over the cooled leeks and all but a small handful of the grated cheese. Fold over the dough to enclose the leeks and cheese and knead for 2–3 minutes, or until the leeks and cheese have been incorporated.

8 Shape the dough into 10 evenly sized rolls and space them out on the prepared baking sheet. Cover loosely with lightly oiled cling film and leave to prove for 20–30 minutes. Meanwhile, heat the oven to 220°C/gas mark 7.

9 Beat the egg with a fork, sieve it and brush carefully over buns. Bake in the top third of the oven for 20–30 minutes, then remove from the oven, brush the buns with a little milk and sprinkle with the remaining grated cheese.

10 Return to the oven and bake for a further 5 minutes, or until the cheese has melted and is golden brown. Transfer the buns to a wire rack to cool.

ENGLISH BUTTERMILK MUFFINS

MAKES 10	
150ml milk	1 tsp salt
15g fresh yeast	100ml buttermilk (see note on page 88)
2 tbsp tepid water	
½ tsp caster sugar	Oil, to grease
1 egg	Rice flour, to dust
500g strong plain flour, plus extra to dust	

English muffins are delicious served hot from the oven with butter or split in half and toasted for breakfast. For a classic eggs Benedict, split and toast the muffins, then top with a poached egg and hollandaise sauce.

1 Pour the milk into a small pan and bring to scalding point (see page 155) over a medium heat. Remove from the heat and leave to cool to tepid, about 38°C.

2 In a small bowl, cream together the yeast, water and sugar. Beat the egg in another bowl.

3 Put the flour and salt in a large bowl and make a well in the middle. Pour in the egg and buttermilk and add the yeast mixture, taking care to scrape all the yeast in. Add two thirds of the milk. Stir with a cutlery knife, then with your hands, adding enough of the reserved milk to make a soft but not sticky dough.

4 Turn the dough out onto a very lightly floured surface and knead for about 8–10 minutes (see page 12) until soft and elastic. Place the ball of dough in a lightly oiled bowl, turning to coat it lightly. Cover with lightly oiled cling film and leave to rise in a warm place for about 1 hour until doubled in size.

5 Roll the dough out to a 2cm thickness, without kneading again. Sprinkle the work surface with a fine layer of rice flour, then lift the dough onto it and sprinkle with another fine layer of rice flour. Cut out 10 muffins, using an 8cm floured cutter.

6 Place the muffins on a large, oiled baking sheet, leaving plenty of space for them to expand as they rise. Gently cover with lightly oiled cling film and leave to prove to 1½ times their original thickness, about 1 hour. Heat the oven to 180°C/gas mark 4.

7 Heat a large non-stick frying pan over a medium heat and cook the muffins in batches for 3–5 minutes each side. You may need to turn the heat down to prevent them from scorching. Transfer the muffins to another baking sheet.

8 When all the muffins have been fried, bake in the oven for 10–15 minutes until cooked through. Transfer the cooked muffins to a wire rack to cool and loosely wrap in a clean tea towel to keep the crusts soft. Serve split in half, with butter.

TARALLI PUGLIESI

MAKES 8–10

250g '00' flour, plus extra
   to dust
½ tsp salt
3g fast-action dried yeast
1 tsp fennel seeds

100ml white wine
65ml olive oil
A little tepid water, to mix
   (optional)

These are a favourite snack throughout Southern Italy. They are shaped and cooked a little like bagels, but with a much more rustic and free-form shape. They make a lovely accompaniment to a meal. The '00' flour used here (though more commonly in pasta) is high in gluten, but is milled much more finely than strong white bread flour, so it gives a finer texture.

1 Mix the flour and salt together in a medium bowl, then sprinkle in the yeast.

2 In a small, dry frying pan, lightly toast the fennel seeds over a low heat for 2 minutes until fragrant, then remove from the pan and gently bruise with a rolling pin or pestle and mortar, without crushing them.

3 Add the toasted fennel seeds to the flour and pour in the wine and oil. Mix to a soft but not sticky dough; it should be a little firmer than a normal bread dough, but you may still need to add a few tbsp of tepid water.

4 Knead by hand for about 10 minutes (see page 12) or in an electric mixer fitted with a dough hook for 5 minutes until smooth and elastic. Place in a lightly oiled bowl, cover with lightly oiled cling film and leave to rise for 45–60 minutes, or until increased in size by at least a third.

5 Heat the oven to 200°C/gas mark 6. Line a large baking sheet with baking parchment. Fill a medium pan two thirds full with water and bring to the boil. Place a clean, dry tea towel on a tray next to the pan.

6 Turn the dough out onto a floured surface and divide into 8–10 equal portions. Roll each into a baton, about 15cm long. Loop each one into a ring with the ends slightly overlapping, then press your thumb firmly on the overlapping edge to seal.

7 Lower 2 taralli into the boiling water at a time. Wait for them to almost come to the surface, then remove to the tea towel to dry, using a slotted spoon, and repeat with the rest.

8 Once all the taralli are poached, place on the baking sheet and bake in the oven for 20–25 minutes until golden brown. Transfer to a wire rack and leave to cool before serving.

FRESH HERB NAAN BREADS

| MAKES 8 |

150–200ml milk
20g butter or ghee
15g fresh yeast
1 tsp caster sugar
450g strong white flour
1 tsp salt

1 tbsp nigella or black
    onion seeds
150g plain yoghurt
Few coriander, mint and
    flat-leaf parsley sprigs
Oil, to grease

The inclusion of lots of herbs in these naan breads gives them a wonderful fresh flavour. If you freeze the naans at the end of step 4, they can be defrosted, risen and cooked whenever you need them.

1 Pour the milk into a small saucepan and bring to scalding point (see page 155) over a medium heat. Remove from the heat, add the butter or ghee and allow to melt. Allow to cool until tepid, about 38°C.

2 In a small bowl, mix the yeast with a spoonful or two of the tepid milk, then stir in the sugar. Mix the flour and salt in a large bowl and stir in the nigella seeds. Add the yeast mixture, yoghurt and three quarters of the milk and melted butter mix. Mix thoroughly, adding enough of the remaining milk to make a soft dough.

3 Tip out onto the work surface and knead the dough for 10 minutes (see page 12) until smooth and elastic. Roughly chop a mixture of the herbs, so you have about 3 tbsp in total, and knead them into the dough. Place in a lightly oiled bowl, cover with lightly oiled cling film and leave to rise in a warm place for about 1 hour, or until doubled in size.

4 Divide the dough into 8 equal pieces and roll each piece into a large oval, about 3mm thick. Make sure the dough is not thicker than this, or it will not have a chance to cook through in the pan before the outside becomes too dark. You may need to rest the dough from time to time while rolling as it may become quite elastic and difficult to roll.

5 Lay the rolled breads on a lightly oiled tray or work surface and cover with lightly oiled cling film. Leave to prove for about 15 minutes, or until they are visibly rising again and about 5mm thick. Heat the oven to 120°C/gas mark ½.

6 Heat a heavy-based frying pan over a medium heat and brush it with oil. Working in batches according to the size of the pan, brush the top of each naan with water and fry for 3 minutes before turning it and brushing the other side with water. Fry the second side for 3 minutes, or until well browned.

7 Keep warm in a low oven while you cook the remaining breads. Serve warm with curries, or cut into slices and served with Indian spiced dips.

SPICED CHICKPEA FLAT BREADS

MAKES 8–10

1 tbsp cumin seeds
1 tbsp coriander seeds
Large handful of coriander
  leaves
15g fresh yeast
10g caster sugar
300ml tepid water

450g strong white flour,
  plus extra to dust
15g salt
400g tin chickpeas,
  drained and rinsed
Oil, to grease

These easy-to-make spicy flat breads are lovely served alongside curries, or as an accompaniment to Middle Eastern style mezze.

1 Toast the cumin and coriander seeds in a dry frying pan over a low to medium heat until lightly toasted. Tip them out onto a plate and allow to cool, then crush with a pestle and mortar or in a small bowl using the end of a rolling pin. Coarsely chop the coriander leaves.

2 In a small bowl, mix the yeast, sugar and 2 tbsp of the water together. Mix the flour and salt in a large bowl, add the yeast mixture and enough of the water to make a soft but not sloppy dough, using a little of the water to swill out the yeast bowl. Knead the dough for 3 minutes (see page 12) until smooth.

3 Blend the chickpeas to a rough paste in a food processor, then stir in the crushed cumin and coriander seeds.

4 Mix the chickpea and spice mixture and chopped coriander into the dough and knead for another couple of minutes, or until springy and elastic. Place in a lightly oiled bowl, cover with lightly oiled cling film and leave to rise until doubled in size, about 1 hour. Meanwhile, heat the oven to 230°C/gas mark 8, with 2 baking sheets inside.

5 Divide the risen dough into 8–10 pieces and roll out each one on a floured surface to a rough oval, about 2.5mm thick. As you shape them, cover with a damp tea towel to prevent them from drying out.

6 Transfer the flat breads to the heated baking sheets and bake in the oven for 15 minutes, then turn them over and return to the oven for 5–10 minutes, or until risen a little and golden, with no grey patches of uncooked dough. Serve warm.

PITTA BREAD

MAKES 10–12

15g fresh yeast
250–280ml tepid water
1 tsp caster sugar
375g strong white flour, plus
    extra if needed and to dust

1¼ tsp salt
Oil, to grease

It is worth investing in a non-stick baking sheet as it allows the pitta breads to be cooked without oil, giving the traditional dry finish, rather than a 'fried' exterior. They can also be cooked in a dry frying pan on the hob, in batches.

1 Dissolve the yeast in 100ml of the tepid water and stir in the sugar. Set aside for 10–15 minutes until frothy.

2 Sift the flour and salt into a large bowl. Pour the yeast mixture over the flour, add another 150ml tepid water and stir the liquid into the flour. Add a little more water or flour as necessary to create a soft, sticky dough. Stir the dough well with a wooden spoon until well combined and a little elastic.

3 Transfer the dough to a lightly floured surface and knead for about 10 minutes (see page 12) until it is less sticky, smooth and elastic.

4 Put the dough into an oiled bowl and turn it over so it is fully coated with oil. Cover with cling film and leave the dough to rise in a warm place until doubled in size, about 1 hour.

5 Place the risen dough on a lightly floured surface and roll it out into a long sausage. Cut the dough into 10–12 equal pieces and roll each piece into a ball. Cover with lightly oiled cling film and leave to rest for 10 minutes.

6 Meanwhile, heat the oven to 250°C/gas mark 10 and place a large baking sheet in the bottom third of the oven to heat up.

7 Roll out each ball of dough into a circle or slipper shape, about 5mm thick.

8 Cook the pitta breads in batches as they are rolled. Bake for about 5 minutes until they have puffed up, then turn the pittas over and bake for a further 2–3 minutes until cooked, with no sign of grey uncooked dough.

9 Remove the pitta breads from the oven and serve warm. Any unused pittas can be wrapped and frozen, to be defrosted and reheated when required.

PRETZELS

MAKES 6

310g strong white flour,
   plus extra to dust
25g caster sugar
1½ tsp salt
2 tsp fast-action dried yeast
½ tbsp light olive oil, plus
   extra to grease

180ml tepid water
Semolina, to sprinkle
   (or use flour)
50g bicarbonate of soda
1 litre boiling water
25g salt flakes or large
   crystals

The distinctive shape of a pretzel is said to represent hands in prayer. Pretzels are traditionally finished with salt flakes, but a sprinkling of seeds or nuts could be applied instead. Flavourings such as caraway or onion seeds can be added to the dough as well, if you like. Dipping the pretzel in the alkali solution before baking causes the crust to take on its deep brown colour. The pretzels can also be given an egg glaze before sprinkling with salt and baking, for a shiny finish.

1 Mix the flour, sugar and salt in a large bowl, then sprinkle in the yeast and stir thoroughly. Add the oil and three quarters of the tepid water and mix until the dough is soft but not sticky, adding more water if you need to.

2 Turn the dough out onto a lightly oiled surface and knead for 8–10 minutes (see page 12) until smooth and elastic. (Or you can knead the dough in a mixer fitted with a dough hook for 4–5 minutes.)

3 Place the dough in a lightly oiled bowl, cover with lightly oiled cling film and leave to rise until doubled in size, 1–2 hours.

4 Heat the oven to 220°C/gas mark 7 and sprinkle a baking sheet with semolina. Put the bicarbonate of soda in a jug, pour on the boiling water and stir. Place a clean, dry tea towel next to the jug.

5 Turn out the risen dough onto a lightly floured surface and divide into 6 even pieces. Cover all but one with lightly oiled cling film, and roll one piece into a rope, 55–60cm long. You may need to start rolling one rope, then, as it becomes elastic and springs back, put it aside and start on another, then come back to the first, which will have relaxed a little and will be easier to roll. Repeat with all the pieces of dough, then twist each into a pretzel shape (as shown).

6 Once they have all been shaped, dip each pretzel into the hot water and bicarbonate of soda solution, then remove with an oiled slotted spoon or spider strainer to the tea towel to drain.

7 Transfer to the baking sheet, sprinkle with the salt flakes and bake in the oven for 12–15 minutes until dark golden. Cool on a wire rack.

Variation

✽ **Cinnamon and raisin pretzels** For delicious sweet pretzels, flavour the dough with ground cinnamon to taste, adding it to the flour with the salt and sugar. Incorporate a handful of raisins into the dough as you knead it. After baking and cooling, dust the pretzels with icing sugar or drizzle with glacé icing for a decorative finish.

PARMESAN GRISSINI

MAKES 15–18	
50g Parmesan cheese	1 tsp salt
7g fresh yeast	1 tbsp olive oil, plus extra
150ml tepid water	to grease
2 tsp caster sugar	1 egg
225g strong white flour,	1 tbsp sesame seeds
plus extra to dust	or Maldon sea salt

Grissini are cooked at a much lower temperature than other breads, as the aim is for crisp breadsticks that have pretty much dried out inside. They have a close, light texture and so are not risen for long. Don't try to make them all look uniform – they are most appealing if the shape and length is irregular. For plain grissini, simply leave out the Parmesan.

1 Heat the oven to 150°C/gas mark 2. Finely grate the Parmesan. In a small bowl, dissolve the yeast in 3 tbsp of the water then stir in the sugar.

2 Mix the flour and salt in a large bowl, stir in the grated Parmesan, then pour in the yeast mixture, oil and enough of the water to make a soft but not sticky dough.

3 Tip the dough onto a floured surface and knead for 5 minutes (see page 12) until starting to become smooth and elastic. Place in a lightly oiled bowl, cover with lightly oiled cling film and leave to relax for 10 minutes.

4 Remove the dough from the bowl, roll it out into a rectangle, about 30 x 20cm, then cut it into 15–18 strips. Using your fingers, roll each strip of dough out into a thin sausage, about 1cm in diameter. Lay them on 2 oiled baking sheets, cover with lightly oiled cling film and leave to prove for 10–15 minutes, or until increased in size by half again.

5 Beat the egg in a bowl using a fork, then sieve it. Carefully brush the grissini with beaten egg, sprinkle with sesame seeds or salt flakes and bake in the oven for about 45 minutes until golden brown and crisp through. Cool on a wire rack.

4

QUICK BREADS

This is the chapter to turn to when you haven't enough time to allow yeast to work its magic. Many of these recipes can be prepared, baked (and eaten!) well within an hour, so try one of the tempting savoury scones, a pan-fried potato farl or a spicy muffin to transform a simple bowl of soup or a salad into a more exciting lunch.

SODA BREAD

MAKES 1 medium loaf

250g plain flour, plus extra
   to dust
250g wholemeal flour
1½ tsp salt

2 tsp bicarbonate of soda
1 tbsp caster sugar
50g butter
300–350ml buttermilk

Soda bread is best made on the day you are going to eat it, although leftover slices can be toasted or even made into breadcrumbs. It is perfect cut into wedges and served with lashings of salty butter.

1 Heat the oven to 190°C/gas mark 5. Lightly flour a large baking sheet.

2 Sift the flours, salt, bicarbonate of soda and sugar into a large bowl and add back any bran still left in the sieve.

3 Cut the butter into 1cm pieces and rub into the flour mixture with your fingertips, then briskly stir in just enough buttermilk to make a soft dough.

4 Transfer the dough to the floured baking sheet and shape, with a minimum of handling, into a large disc about 4–5cm thick. With the floured handle of a wooden spoon, mark a 2cm deep cross on top (as shown), then lightly dust with flour.

5 Bake in the oven for 35–45 minutes until the soda bread is risen, golden brown and with no greyness evident in the cross. Remove to a wire rack to cool.

A note on buttermilk...

✱ If you cannot find buttermilk, use milk and add 2 tsp cream of tartar to the dry ingredients. Alternatively, add 2–3 tbsp lemon juice to ordinary milk and leave in a warm place for 10–15 minutes to sour the milk, which will provide enough acidity for the dough.

Variation

✱ **Fruited white soda bread** Use all white flour and add an extra 6 tbsp sugar to the flour, with 175g raisins or sultanas.

CHEESY SODA FARLS

MAKES 4	
225g plain flour, plus extra to dust	¼ tsp salt
½ tsp bicarbonate of soda	30g Parmesan cheese
½ tsp cream of tartar	150–165ml buttermilk (or see note on page 88)
Pinch of cayenne pepper	
¼ tsp English mustard powder	Unsalted butter, melted, to serve

Similar to soda bread in flavour, soda farls are cooked directly over the heat, and served hot, like crumpets or English muffins. Farl is Gaelic for '4 parts', and traditionally the dough is divided into quarters before cooking. However, they can be made in any size or shape; just adjust the cooking time accordingly.

1 Sift the flour, bicarbonate of soda, cream of tartar, cayenne pepper, mustard powder and salt into a large bowl. Grate the Parmesan and stir into the dry mixture.

2 Make a well in the centre and pour in 150ml buttermilk. Using a cutlery knife, mix to a soft, spongy dough, adding a little more buttermilk if necessary. Remove to a lightly floured surface and knead gently for 30 seconds to 1 minute until just smooth; don't over-work the dough or the cooked farls will be heavy and poorly risen.

3 Flour a rolling pin and roll the dough into a circle about ¾–1cm thick. Using a large, sharp knife dipped into a little flour to prevent it from sticking, cut into quarters.

4 Put a frying pan over a medium heat and dust with a little flour. Lay the farls in the floured pan and cook for 5–6 minutes until the bottoms are lightly browned, checking regularly to make sure they are not catching around the edges. Turn them over, using a fish slice, and cook for a further 5–6 minutes, or until cooked through. If your pan is not large enough and you need to cook these in batches, heat your oven to 180°C/gas mark 4 and your first batch can finish cooking in the oven once browned, while you cook the second batch in the pan.

5 Brush with plenty of melted butter and serve hot from the pan or oven.

SMOKED PAPRIKA CORNBREAD

MAKES 1 small loaf

1 tbsp sunflower oil,
   plus extra to grease
75g self-raising flour
75g fine polenta
1 tsp baking powder

½ tsp salt
¼ tsp smoked paprika
150g Greek yoghurt
1 egg

Like the soda bread on page 88, this is a quick bread, raised with baking powder rather than yeast. It has a distinctive smoky flavour and is great served with a chowder or other hearty soups. This mixture can also be baked in 6 muffin cases, allowing 15–20 minutes in the oven. You will need a 450–500g loaf tin.

1 Heat the oven to 180°C/gas mark 4. Line the base of the loaf tin with a piece of non-stick baking parchment and lightly oil the sides.

2 Sift the flour, polenta, baking powder, salt and smoked paprika into a bowl.

3 In a separate bowl, whisk together the sunflower oil, yoghurt and egg. Make a well in the middle of the dry mixture and pour in the wet ingredients. Beat well with a wooden spoon until you have a smooth but thick batter-like mixture.

4 Pour the mixture into the prepared tin and bake on the middle shelf of the oven for 30–35 minutes, or until a skewer inserted into the middle comes out clean.

5 Remove from the oven and leave the cornbread in the tin for a minute before removing, peeling off the paper and transferring to a wire rack to cool.

QUICK CHILLI BREAD

MAKES 1 small loaf

4 tbsp olive oil, plus extra to grease
1 red chilli
1 green chilli
35g Parmesan cheese
225g plain flour
1 tbsp baking powder

½ tsp salt
110g fine polenta
1 tbsp caster sugar
1 egg
150ml crème fraîche
150ml milk

As this bread doesn't require kneading or a rising period, it is quick and easy to make. Just make sure you put it into the oven as soon as the ingredients are mixed – to ensure it achieves the best possible rise. You will need a 450–500g loaf tin.

1 Heat the oven to 180°C/gas mark 4. Line the base of the loaf tin with greaseproof paper, then lightly oil the base and sides.

2 Cut the chillies in half, remove the stalks, seeds and white membranes and then finely chop. Finely grate the Parmesan.

3 Sift the flour, baking powder and salt into a large bowl. Stir in the polenta, sugar and chopped chillies. Stir in 3 tbsp of the grated Parmesan.

4 In a separate bowl, beat the egg and then beat in the oil, crème fraîche and milk. Swiftly stir the wet mixture into the dry ingredients, using a spatula or wooden spoon. Avoid over-mixing or the bread will lose air bubbles and not rise as well.

5 Scrape the mixture into the prepared tin and sprinkle with the remaining Parmesan. Bake on the middle shelf of the oven for 45–60 minutes until well risen and lightly browned.

6 Leave the loaf to rest in the tin for 5 minutes, then remove and transfer to a wire rack. Peel off the greaseproof paper and leave to cool slightly. Serve warm.

CORNBREAD MUFFINS
WITH OLIVES, LEMON AND THYME

MAKES 8	
1 large lemon	1 tbsp baking powder
Few thyme sprigs	1 tsp salt
60g pitted black olives	300ml buttermilk (or
60g feta cheese	see note on page 88)
60g Parmesan cheese	50ml milk
180g plain flour	1 large egg
100g quick cook polenta	

These savoury muffins have a punchy, piquant flavour. You will need a 12-hole muffin tin, lined with 8 paper muffin cases.

1 Heat the oven to 220°C/gas mark 7. Finely grate the lemon zest and finely chop enough thyme leaves to give you 1 tsp. Roughly chop the black olives and cut the feta into small cubes, about 1cm. Grate the Parmesan.

2 Sift the flour, polenta, baking powder and salt together into a large bowl. Stir in the cheeses, olives, lemon zest and thyme.

3 Beat the buttermilk, milk and egg together in a small bowl and quickly stir the wet mixture into the dry ingredients to form a soft, dropping consistency. Add a little more milk if required.

4 Divide the mixture evenly between the 8 muffin cases and bake on the top shelf of the oven for 20–25 minutes, or until a skewer inserted into the middle of a muffin comes out clean. Transfer to a wire rack and allow to cool slightly, or completely, before serving.

WATERCRESS SCONES

MAKES 6

225g self-raising flour,
    plus extra to dust
85g bunch of watercress
½ tsp salt

55g butter
150ml buttermilk (or
    see note on page 88)
1 egg

These scones have a delicious peppery flavour and are perfect for afternoon tea – split in half and topped with cucumber, poached salmon or crab pâté, or with cream cheese, smoked salmon and a squeeze of lime.

1 Heat the oven to 220°C/gas mark 7. Sift a little flour over a large baking sheet.

2 Wash the watercress in cold water, then pat dry with kitchen paper, remove the coarse stalks and finely chop.

3 Sift the flour and salt into a large bowl. Cut the butter into small pieces, then rub it into the flour with your fingertips until the mix resembles breadcrumbs. Stir in the chopped watercress.

4 Make a deep well in the centre of the mixture, add the buttermilk and mix to a soft, spongy dough, using a cutlery knife. The dough may appear to be too dry at this point, but don't worry – the watercress will add moisture.

5 Knead the dough very lightly on a lightly floured surface until just smooth, then bring it into a large round using floured hands. Using a large knife, cut it into 6 wedge-shaped scones. Beat the egg in a small bowl with a fork until well broken up.

6 Arrange the scones on the prepared baking sheet and brush the tops with the beaten egg. Bake in the top of the oven for 20–25 minutes, or until well risen and brown. Remove from the oven and transfer to a wire rack to cool.

GOAT'S CHEESE AND OREGANO SCONE LOAF

MAKES 1 medium loaf	
110g firm goat's cheese	½ tsp salt
1 oregano sprig	55g butter
1 lemon	150ml buttermilk (or
225g self-raising flour,	see note on page 88)
plus extra to dust	1 egg

Serve this scone loaf in thick slices with a Greek salad, or other main course salad for a lovely summer lunch.

1 Heat the oven to 220°C/gas mark 7. Crumble the goat's cheese into a bowl. Finely chop enough oregano to give you 1 tsp, and finely grate the lemon zest; add both to the bowl.

2 Sift the flour and salt into a separate bowl. Cut the butter into small pieces, stir into the flour and rub it in using your fingertips, until the mixture resembles coarse breadcrumbs.

3 Stir in the goat's cheese mixture, then pour in the buttermilk and mix to a soft, spongy dough, using a cutlery knife.

4 Tip the dough onto a floured surface and shape into a round loaf, about 5–6cm thick. Place on a lightly floured baking sheet. Using a large knife, make a lattice pattern on top of the loaf with shallow cuts. In a small bowl, beat the egg and brush it over the top of the loaf.

5 Bake in the oven for 10 minutes, then lower the oven setting to 190°C/gas mark 5 and bake for a further 20–30 minutes, or until the loaf is well browned and cooked through. Remove to a wire rack to cool.

COURGETTE AND CHEESE PICNIC LOAF

MAKES 1 large loaf

85g butter, plus extra
   to grease
110g Cheddar or
   Gruyère cheese
225g courgettes (about
   1 large or 2 small)

225g self-raising flour
½ tsp salt
Pinch of cayenne pepper
3 eggs
55ml milk

This bread is ideal for slicing and taking on a picnic, as it is easy to transport and fairly substantial when served with a selection of salads. You might like to add a handful of chopped fresh soft herbs, such as basil, dill or coriander, along with the grated courgettes. You will need a 900g–1kg loaf tin.

1 Heat the oven to 180°C/gas mark 4. Line the base of the loaf tin with greaseproof paper, then lightly grease the base and sides with butter.

2 Melt the butter in a small saucepan over a gentle heat, then remove from the heat and allow to cool slightly.

3 Grate the cheese on a coarse grater. Wash, trim and grate the courgettes.

4 Sift the flour with the salt and cayenne into a large bowl and stir in the grated cheese.

5 Beat the eggs with the milk. Make a well in the centre of the dry ingredients, add the egg mixture then the melted butter. Mix into the flour, using a wooden spoon, then stir in the grated courgettes.

6 Spoon the mixture into the prepared tin and level the surface. Bake in the oven for 40–50 minutes, or until a skewer inserted into the centre of the loaf comes out clean.

7 Leave to cool a little before removing the loaf from the tin and transferring to a wire rack to cool.

CHILLI AND FETA CORN MUFFINS

MAKES 9	
2–3 green jalapeño chillies, to taste	1 tbsp baking powder
50g feta cheese	Pinch of salt
Small bunch of coriander	30g soft light brown sugar
200g plain flour	90ml water
70g fine yellow cornmeal	3 large eggs
	70ml sunflower oil

The cornmeal gives these muffins a lovely texture and the salty feta, together with the chilli, makes them especially more-ish. You will need a 12-hole muffin tin, lined with 9 paper muffin cases.

1 Heat the oven to 180°C/gas mark 4 and place a baking sheet in the oven to heat up.

2 Halve, deseed and finely chop the chillies, and crumble the feta. Pick the coriander leaves and coarsely chop them.

3 Sift the flour, cornmeal, baking powder and salt together into a large bowl. Add the sugar and stir in the chillies, feta and chopped coriander.

4 In a jug, mix the together the water, eggs and sunflower oil. Add this mixture to the dry ingredients and stir together until just combined; try to avoid over-mixing. Fill each paper case about two thirds full, then place the tin on the heated baking sheet in the oven.

5 Bake in the oven for 15–20 minutes, or until a skewer inserted into the centre of a muffin comes out clean. Leave the muffins to cool in the tin for 5 minutes before transferring to a wire rack to cool slightly. Serve warm.

SWEET APPLE AND RAISIN SODA BREAD

MAKES 2 medium loaves	
50g dried apples	1½ tsp salt
100g large raisins	50g butter
50g hazelnuts	100g caster sugar
225g wholemeal flour	2 tsp bicarbonate of soda
225g plain flour, plus extra to dust	300–350ml buttermilk (or see note on page 88)
2 tsp ground mixed spice	

This is a simple and delicious bread that can be served for tea, but is especially good served with blue cheese.

1 Heat the oven to 190°C/gas mark 5. Using kitchen scissors, chop the dried apples into 1–2cm pieces and put in a small bowl with the raisins. Pour over enough boiling water to just cover the fruit, and set aside to soak for 30 minutes.

2 Meanwhile, spread the hazelnuts out on a baking sheet and roast in the oven for 10 minutes, or until lightly browned. Remove from the baking sheet and set aside to cool.

3 Sift both flours, the mixed spice and salt into a large bowl. Cut the butter into small pieces and rub into the flour using your fingertips until the mixture resembles fine breadcrumbs. Stir in the sugar and bicarbonate of soda.

4 Roughly chop the cooled nuts. Strain the soaked fruit and discard the liquid. Stir the fruit and chopped nuts into the flour mixture.

5 Add enough of the buttermilk to make a soft but not sticky dough. Divide the dough into 2 equal pieces and form into round, slightly domed loaves, about 5cm thick. Place the loaves on a large, lightly floured baking sheet, or on 2 smaller ones.

6 Dip the handle of a wooden spoon in flour and mark a 2cm deep cross on top of each loaf, then lightly dust with flour. Bake in the oven for 40–50 minutes or until well risen, with no evidence of raw dough showing through the cross in the centre.

7 Transfer to a wire rack to cool for at least 15 minutes, but ideally serve while still warm.

PAIN D'ÉPICES

MAKES 1 large loaf

40g unsalted butter
160ml whole milk
275g runny honey
2 eggs
60g caster sugar
Finely grated zest of
  ¼ orange
Finely grated zest of
  ¼ lemon
275g plain flour

60g dark rye flour
2 tsp baking powder
1 tsp ground cinnamon
1 tsp ground ginger
Pinch of freshly grated
  nutmeg
Pinch of ground cloves
Pinch of salt
60g medium oatmeal
¼ tsp anise seeds

Pain d'épices is traditionally served thinly sliced with pâté de foie gras, but it is equally good served with soft cheese, such as fresh young goat's cheese. Alternatively, you can simply eat it buttered, with a cup of tea. You will need a 900g–1kg loaf tin.

1 Heat the oven to 180°C/gas mark 4. Use a little of the butter to grease the tin, then put the remainder in a medium saucepan with the milk and honey. Place over a low heat and stir to melt the honey into the liquid; don't allow the milk to boil. Remove from the heat and pour into a jug to cool.

2 Break the eggs into a medium bowl and add the sugar and citrus zests. Using an electric whisk, beat together until the mixture is pale, light and fluffy. It should be thick enough to leave a ribbon over the surface that holds for 5–6 seconds when the whisk is lifted and some of the mixture falls from it.

3 Sift both flours, the baking powder, ground spices and salt together in a separate bowl. Mix in the oatmeal and anise seeds and make a well in the centre.

4 Spoon the egg mixture into the well and pour in about half of the cooled milk mixture. Use a cutlery knife to distribute the liquid evenly and bring the ingredients together. Add the remaining milk in several additions, stirring well between each addition, until all of the liquid has been incorporated and the batter is smooth and lump-free.

5 Spoon or pour the batter into the prepared tin and bake in the top third of the oven for about 45 minutes, or until risen, golden brown and a skewer inserted into the centre comes away clean, or with a few moist crumbs clinging to it. (You may need to put the loaf on a lower shelf about halfway through cooking if it becomes too dark.)

6 Remove the cooked loaf from the oven and leave it in the tin for about 10 minutes, before turning out onto a wire rack to cool.

5

SWEET AND ENRICHED DOUGHS

Doughs can be enriched with egg and, or, butter to delicious effect – as in the classic French brioche loaf. Adding fat in the form of butter, oil or egg yolk – or adding sugar, alcohol or spices – to a bread dough affects the way the yeast and the gluten work. The yeast will work more slowly, so the process will take longer. Often enriched dough bread recipes use a little more yeast to counterbalance these effects. The fat and sugar also prevents the gluten becoming strong and elastic, so enriched breads are less chewy and have a more tender texture than other breads.

BRIOCHE

MAKES 2 loaves	
85ml milk	**FOR LINING THE MOULD**
20g fresh yeast	30g butter
500g plain flour	Flour, to dust
1½ tsp salt	
30g caster sugar	**FOR THE GLAZE**
6 eggs	1 egg yolk
350g butter, softened	1 tbsp milk

This recipe uses plain flour, which has a lower gluten content than strong bread flour, giving the brioche a cake-like texture. You will need two 450–500g loaf tins. Alternatively, you can bake the dough in a large fluted brioche mould, shaping it as described for individual brioches.

1 Pour the milk into a small saucepan and bring to scalding point (see page 155) over a medium heat. Remove from the heat and cool to tepid, about 38°C. Pour the milk over the yeast in a small bowl and stir to dissolve.

2 Meanwhile, put the flour, salt and sugar in a large bowl. Lightly beat the eggs and add to the flour along with the milk and yeast mixture. Using a cutlery knife, mix to a very soft dough. Then, using a wooden spoon, beat the dough until smooth and elastic, about 10–15 minutes.

3 Turn the dough onto a work surface and, with your fingertips, work the dough by stretching it to shoulder height; it won't stretch this far until the gluten is fully developed, so keep working it until it does.

4 Cut the butter into walnut-sized pieces. Using the same kneading-stretching technique, work the pieces of butter into the dough one at a time, only adding each when the previous piece is completely worked in. As more butter is worked in, the dough should gradually become more shiny, elastic and glossy.

5 Lift the dough into a clean bowl and cover with lightly oiled cling film. Leave to rise in a warm place until doubled in size, about 2 hours.

6 Tip the dough out onto the surface and knock back by turning it over with your fingertips a few times. Refrigerate, covered, for at least 3–4 hours (up to 24 hours).

7 To prepare the tins, melt the 30g butter in a small saucepan and remove from the heat. Brush the loaf tins with the butter and set aside in a cool place for the butter to firm up, then brush again with butter and, before the butter sets the second time, dust with flour, tapping any excess out.

8 Divide the dough in half, shape into 2 loaves (see page 14) and place them in the tins. Cover loosely with lightly oiled cling film and leave to prove at room temperature until risen to the top of the mould. Place in the fridge for 10–15 minutes to firm the dough. Meanwhile, heat the oven to 220°C/gas mark 7.

9 For the glaze, lightly whisk the egg yolk and milk together in a small bowl, then sieve. Brush the risen brioche with the egg glaze, taking care not to let it drip down the sides of the mould.

10 Bake for 40–45 minutes until cooked and dark golden brown on top. Brioche should be quite dark, but if it appears to be colouring too quickly, lower the oven setting to 200°C/gas mark 6. The brioche should come out of the tin easily and sound hollow when tapped on the base. Cool on a wire rack.

To make individual brioches...

Grease and dust 12 small fluted brioche tins. Divide the dough into 12 pieces. To shape the brioche (as illustrated overleaf), roll three quarters of each piece into a ball and place in the tins. Make a hole in the middle of each with a floured wooden spoon handle. Roll the remaining pieces of dough into 12 small balls, place in the holes in the larger rounds, and press the spoon handle through to seal. Place on a tray, cover loosely with cling film and prove as above. Refrigerate as above, then brush with the egg glaze and bake for 8–10 minutes.

STEP 2 Beating the dough with a wooden spoon until smooth and elastic.

STEP 3 Working the dough by stretching it continuously with the fingertips until it can be stretched to shoulder height.

STEP 4 Using the same stretch-kneading technique to incorporate the softened pieces of butter into the dough, one at a time.

STEP 6 Knocking back the risen dough by turning it over with the fingertips a few times.

SHAPING INDIVIDUAL BRIOCHES

1 Making a hole in the larger ball of brioche dough in the individual mould, by pressing the floured handle of a wooden spoon through.

2 Positioning the smaller ball of dough on top of the larger one.

3 Pressing the handle of the wooden spoon down through the middle of the brioche to seal the 2 pieces together.

4 Brushing the brioche with beaten egg and milk to glaze.

APPLE AND CINNAMON BRIOCHE BUNS

MAKES 8

½ quantity brioche dough
  (see page 106)
Flour, to dust
2 sweet dessert apples
1 tbsp lemon juice
75g butter, softened,
  plus extra to grease

50g soft dark brown sugar
1 tsp ground cinnamon

FOR THE CALVADOS GLAZE
100g icing sugar
1–2 tbsp Calvados

In this recipe, brioche dough is swirled with a delicious apple and cinnamon mixture, rather like a decadent Chelsea bun. You can also make individual apple and cinnamon buns, by cooking each bun in a tartlet tin for 10–15 minutes. The brioche dough freezes well, so you could make a whole quantity, use half for this recipe and freeze the other half for another occasion. You will need a 20–22cm round cake tin.

1 Make the brioche dough following the recipe on page 106, up to the end of step 6.

2 While the dough is chilling, peel, core and cut the apples into 5mm dice, then put into a bowl and coat with the lemon juice (the acidity will stop the apple from browning).

3 Place the butter in a medium bowl and beat in the sugar and cinnamon using a wooden spoon.

4 Lift the chilled dough out onto a lightly floured surface. Using a rolling pin, roll the dough to a rectangle about 30 x 25cm, at least 5mm thick. Spread the butter mixture over the dough as evenly as possible, leaving a 5mm border around the edge.

5 Drain the apples and pat dry with kitchen paper. Sprinkle the apple pieces evenly over the spiced butter. Roll up the dough rectangle lengthways as you would for a Swiss roll, trim off the ends and cut into 8 equal slices.

6 Generously grease the cake tin with butter. Arrange 7 buns, cut side up, around the edge of the tin, leaving a little space between each one to allow them to expand as they prove. Place the eighth bun in the middle.

7 Cover loosely with lightly oiled cling film and leave to prove until doubled in size. Meanwhile, heat the oven to 220°C/gas mark 7.

8 Bake in the oven for 40–50 minutes until risen and golden, and without any greyness of uncooked dough towards the centre of each roll. If the brioche starts to take on too much colour before it is cooked, turn the oven down to 180°C/gas mark 4 and continue cooking on a lower shelf. Remove from the oven and turn out onto a wire rack to cool.

9 For the glaze, mix the icing sugar with the Calvados to make a smooth icing and spoon over the brioche.

BANANA AND DATE BRIOCHE BUNS

MAKES 12

250g butter, softened,
   plus 20g to grease
3 over-ripe bananas
1½ tsp vanilla extract
200g pitted Medjool dates
100ml milk, plus 1 tbsp
   to glaze

15g fresh yeast
500g plain flour, plus extra
   to dust
1½ tsp salt
30g soft light brown sugar
3 eggs, plus 1 extra yolk
5 brown sugar lumps

A rich brioche dough is the perfect medium for the mellow flavours of bananas, dates and vanilla. You will need a 12-hole deep muffin tin.

1 Melt the 20g of the butter and use to generously grease the muffin tin.

2 Peel and mash the bananas well using a fork, then stir in the vanilla. Roughly chop the dates and set aside. Put the 100ml milk in a small saucepan over a low heat and warm gently to tepid, no hotter than 38°C. Put the yeast into a small bowl, pour on a few tbsp of the milk and stir to dissolve.

3 Sift the flour and salt into a large bowl and stir in the sugar. Beat the eggs lightly and add to the flour along with the mashed bananas, yeast and remaining warmed milk. Mix, using a cutlery knife, until a very soft dough forms.

4 Using a wooden spoon or an electric food mixer fitted with a dough hook on a low speed, beat the dough until smooth and elastic; this can take about 15 minutes by hand, or 5 minutes by machine.

5 Turn the dough out onto a work surface and, using your fingertips, work the dough by stretching it to shoulder height (as shown on page 107); it won't stretch this far until the gluten is fully developed, so keep working it until it does.

6 Divide the 250g butter into walnut-sized pieces. Work each piece of butter into the dough completely before adding the next piece, using the same kneading technique. The dough should gradually become more shiny, elastic and glossy as more butter is worked in.

7 Knead in the dates until just distributed, then lift the dough into a clean bowl and cover with lightly oiled cling film. Leave to rise in a warm place for 2 hours, or until doubled in size.

8 Knock back the dough by flipping it with your fingertips just a few times, then refrigerate, covered, for several hours, but not more than 24 hours.

9 Shape the brioche dough while it is still very cold. Divide it into 12 equal pieces, shape each into a ball and place in the prepared muffin tin. (You may need to use a little extra flour if the dough becomes too sticky to handle.) Cover loosely with lightly oiled cling film and leave at room temperature to rise to half their size again, then transfer the tin to the fridge for 10–15 minutes to firm the butter.

10 Meanwhile, heat the oven to 220°C/gas mark 7. Put the egg yolk in a small bowl, add the 1 tbsp milk and beat together using a fork. Crush the sugar lumps into small crystal clumps.

11 Brush the brioche with the egg glaze, taking care not to let it drip down the sides. Sprinkle with the crushed sugar and bake in the oven for 10 minutes. Lower the oven setting to 190°C/gas mark 5 and bake for a further 5 minutes, or until the buns are golden brown, sound hollow when tapped on the underside and feel light for their size. Transfer to a wire rack to cool.

CHELSEA BUNS

MAKES 8 large buns

250ml milk
20g fresh yeast
100g caster sugar
500g strong plain flour,
   plus extra to dust
½ tsp salt
100g butter, at room
   temperature, plus extra
   to grease

1 egg
Oil, to grease
1 tsp ground mixed spice
50g sultanas
50g currants
Apricot glaze (see below),
   to finish

The aroma of these buns as they bake is so enticing. The sticky apricot glaze gives them a lovely sheen but you can drizzle glacé icing over the buns instead if you prefer. You will need a 24cm round cake tin.

1 Pour the milk into a saucepan and bring to scalding point (see page 155) over a medium heat, then remove from the heat and leave to cool to tepid, about 38°C.

2 In a small bowl, cream the yeast with 1 tsp of the sugar and 1 tbsp of the milk.

3 Put the flour and salt in a large bowl. Cut 75g of the butter into cubes and rub into the flour with your fingertips. Stir in 50g sugar and make a well in the middle. Set aside the remaining butter in a warm place to soften.

4 Break the egg into a small bowl and beat with a fork. Add the beaten egg to the well in the flour mixture, along with the creamed yeast mixture and at least three quarters of the remaining milk. Using a cutlery knife, bring the dough together, adding any remaining milk if needed to make a soft dough.

5 Transfer the dough to a very lightly floured surface and knead for about 5–8 minutes (see page 12) until smooth.

6 Place the dough in a very lightly oiled bowl and cover with lightly oiled cling film. Leave to rise in a warm place until doubled in size, about 1½ hours.

7 Meanwhile, mix the remaining butter and sugar to a smooth paste with the mixed spice.

8 Transfer the risen dough to the work surface and knock it back, kneading it for 2–3 minutes. Using a rolling pin, roll the dough into a 25cm square. Spread the butter, sugar and spice paste over the dough as evenly as possible, and almost to the edges, then scatter over the dried fruit. Roll the dough up into a Swiss roll, trim off the ends and cut into 8 slices, 3cm thick.

9 Generously grease the cake tin with butter. Arrange 7 buns, cut side up, around the inside edge of the prepared cake tin, leaving a little space between each to allow them to expand as they prove. Place the eighth bun in the middle.

10 Cover loosely with oiled cling film and leave to prove for 25–30 minutes, or until almost doubled in size. Meanwhile, heat the oven to 200°C/gas mark 6.

11 Bake in the oven for 25–35 minutes until risen and golden. Check between the layers for any greyness and bake for a little longer if there is any, on a lower shelf to avoid over-browning. Remove from the oven and lift the whole crown out of the tin onto a wire rack. Brush with apricot glaze and leave to cool.

To make an apricot glaze...

Put 250g apricot jam (not whole fruit) into a small pan with a finely pared strip or two of lemon zest and heat gently, without stirring, until the jam has melted, without letting it boil. If the jam is very thick add 2–3 tbsp warm water to loosen it, then pass through a fine sieve into a bowl, discarding the zest.

HOT CROSS BUNS

MAKES 8	
100ml milk	Oil, to grease
10g fresh yeast	50g currants
2 tbsp tepid water	1 tbsp chopped mixed peel
30g caster sugar	
1 egg	**FOR THE CROSSES**
250g strong plain flour,	**AND GLAZE**
plus extra to dust	50g plain flour
¼ tsp salt	Pinch of baking powder
2–3 tsp ground mixed spice	2 tsp oil
40g butter, at room	15–30ml milk
temperature	1 tsp caster sugar

You can vary the dried fruit for this traditional Easter recipe: chopped dried apricots, dried cranberries, dried cherries or dried dates would all work well in place of the currants and chopped peel.

1 Pour the milk into a saucepan and bring to scalding point (see page 155) over a medium heat, then remove from the heat and leave to cool to tepid, about 38°C.

2 In a small bowl, mix the yeast with the water and ½ tsp of the sugar to create a loose paste. Beat the egg and add it to the yeast mixture.

3 Put the flour, salt and mixed spice in a large bowl. Cut the butter into cubes and rub it into the flour with your fingertips. Stir in the remaining sugar.

4 Make a well in the centre and pour in the yeast mixture and three quarters of the milk, making sure all the yeast is scraped into the well. Stir with a cutlery knife, then with your fingers, adding enough of the reserved milk to make a soft but not sticky dough.

5 Tip the dough out onto a very lightly floured surface and knead for about 8–10 minutes (see page 12) until smooth and elastic, using as little extra flour on the work surface as possible.

6 Place the dough in a very lightly oiled bowl and cover with lightly oiled cling film or a damp tea towel. Leave in a warm place to rise for about 1½ hours until doubled in size.

7 Transfer the risen dough to the work surface and knock it back, kneading for 2–3 minutes and adding in the currants and peel (trying to keep the currants and pieces of peel whole).

8 Divide the dough into 8 equal pieces, shape into rolls (see page 67) and place about 2cm apart on a large, oiled baking sheet. Flatten each slightly with the palm of your hand, then cover with oiled cling film and leave to prove until doubled in size. Meanwhile, heat the oven to 200°C/gas mark 6.

9 To make the crosses, sift the flour and baking powder into a bowl. Stir in the oil and enough cold water to make a thick but pipeable paste. Put into a piping bag fitted with a 5mm nozzle. Once the buns have risen, mix the milk with the sugar and use to lightly brush the buns. Using a sharp knife, cut a shallow 1mm deep cross in the top of each bun and pipe a cross on top.

10 Bake in the oven for 15 minutes then brush the buns again with the sweetened milk and return to the oven for 5 minutes, or until golden brown. They should feel light and sound hollow when tapped on the base. Transfer to a wire rack to cool and serve fresh with butter, or split in half and toasted.

A note on glazing...

✳ For extra shine, brush the cooked, cooled buns with a light sugar syrup (see page 152), in place of the milk glaze.

CINNAMON PECAN TOFFEE BUNS

MAKES 8 large buns

250ml milk
20g fresh yeast
100g caster sugar
500g strong plain flour, plus
    extra to dust
½ tsp salt

175g butter, at room
    temperature
1 egg
Oil, to grease
½–1 tsp ground cinnamon
75g soft light brown sugar
100g pecan nuts

These delicious spiral buns are made in the same way as Chelsea buns (see page 112). As their caramel juices cool, they become irresistibly chewy and toffee-like. Serve them as part of a brunch, or simply with a cup of coffee. You will need a 24cm round cake tin.

1 Pour the milk into a saucepan and bring to scalding point (see page 155) over a medium heat, then remove from the heat and leave to cool to tepid, about 38°C.

2 In a small bowl, cream the yeast with 1 tsp of the caster sugar and 1 tbsp of the milk.

3 Put the flour and salt in a large bowl. Cut 75g of the butter into cubes and rub into the flour with your fingertips. Stir in 50g caster sugar and make a well in the middle. Set aside the remaining butter in a warm place to soften.

4 Break the egg into a small bowl and beat with a fork. Add the beaten egg to the well with the creamed yeast mixture and at least three quarters of the remaining milk. Using a cutlery knife, bring the dough together, adding any remaining milk if needed to make a soft dough.

5 Transfer the dough to a very lightly floured surface and knead for about 5–8 minutes (see page 12) until smooth.

6 Place the dough in a very lightly oiled bowl and cover with lightly oiled cling film. Leave to rise in a warm place until doubled in size, about 1½ hours.

7 Meanwhile, mix 75g of the remaining butter with the rest of the caster sugar and cinnamon to taste, to make a smooth paste.

8 Transfer the risen dough to the work surface and knock it back, kneading it for 2–3 minutes. Using a rolling pin, roll the dough into a 25cm square. Spread the buttery cinnamon paste over the dough as evenly as possible, and almost to the edges. Roll the dough up into a Swiss roll, trim off the ends and cut into 8 slices, 3cm thick.

9 Mix the remaining 25g butter with the soft brown sugar and spread the mixture evenly in the bottom of the cake tin. Roughly chop the pecan nuts and scatter over the butter and sugar layer.

10 Arrange 7 buns, cut side up, around the inside edge of the prepared cake tin, leaving a little space between each to allow them to expand as they prove. Put the eighth bun in the middle.

11 Cover loosely with oiled cling film and leave to prove for 25–30 minutes, or until almost doubled in size. Meanwhile, heat the oven to 200°C/gas mark 6.

12 Bake in the oven for 25–35 minutes until risen and golden. Check between the layers for any greyness and continue to cook a little longer if there is any, on a lower shelf to prevent them taking on too much colour. Remove from the oven and leave to cool slightly.

13 Remove the buns from the tin while they are still warm (or they may stick) and serve upside down, pecan side uppermost. The pecan, butter and sugar mixture will have created a lovely nutty, sticky glaze.

STOLLEN BUNS

MAKES 12

350ml milk
500g strong white flour
1 tsp caster sugar
15g fresh yeast
40g whole blanched almonds
1 orange
1 tsp salt
100g butter
100g raisins
100g sultanas

30g dried cherries or
    cranberries
1 egg
Oil, to grease
120g white marzipan

FOR THE TOPS
25g butter, melted
60g smooth apricot jam
1 tbsp water
2 tbsp crunchy pearl sugar

These mini versions of the classic Christmas sweet bread have a nugget of marzipan hidden in the middle. Crushed sugar cubes work just as well as the pearled sugar on top. You will need a 12-hole muffin tin.

1 Pour the milk into a small saucepan and bring to scalding point (see page 155) over a medium heat. Remove from the heat and allow to cool to tepid, about 38°C.

2 In a large bowl, mix together 100g of the flour, the sugar, yeast and tepid milk. Set aside at warm room temperature until frothy. Meanwhile, roughly chop the almonds and finely grate enough orange zest to give you 2 tsp.

3 Mix the remaining flour and salt in a medium bowl. Cut the butter into small pieces, stir into the flour and rub in with your fingertips. Stir in the chopped almonds, all the dried fruit and the orange zest.

4 Break the egg into a small bowl and beat lightly with a fork to break it up. Stir it into the frothing yeast batter along with the flour and dried fruit mixture. Mix everything together to a soft but not too sticky dough.

5 Tip the dough onto the work surface and knead for about 10 minutes (see page 12) until smooth and elastic. Try not to add more flour as you knead if you can avoid it.

6 Place the dough in a large, lightly oiled bowl and cover with lightly oiled cling film. Leave to rise until doubled in size, about 2 hours.

7 Line the muffin tin with muffin cases, preferably a sturdy large brown paper variety. Divide the marzipan into 12 equal pieces and roll each piece into a ball.

8 Knock the dough back and knead briefly again for 2 minutes. Divide into 24 pieces and push a piece into the base of each muffin case. Place a marzipan ball on each, then cover with the remaining pieces of dough, pressing gently to seal the 2 layers of dough together. Loosely drape a piece of lightly oiled cling film over the top and leave to prove until they have increased in size by half again, about 1 hour. Meanwhile, heat the oven to 190°C/gas mark 5.

9 Brush the tops with melted butter and bake in the oven for 20–25 minutes, or until well browned. Remove the buns in their cases from the tin and allow to cool on a wire rack.

10 Before serving, melt the apricot jam with the 1 tbsp water and use to brush the tops of the buns. Sprinkle with a little crunchy pearl sugar.

HONEY AND FIG CHALLAH

MAKES 1 large plaited loaf

15g fresh yeast
100g runny honey
150ml tepid water
85g dried figs
80ml olive oil
2 eggs, plus 1 extra yolk
525g strong white flour,
    plus extra to dust

1½ tsp salt
Oil, to grease

FOR THE GLAZE
1 egg
1 tbsp granulated sugar

. . . .

This is a delicious variation on the traditional plain enriched challah loaf. Traditionally challah loaves are plaited using 6 strands, but here only 4 strands are plaited to make the finished loaf simpler to achieve.

1 Dissolve the yeast and 1 tsp of the honey in the tepid water in a medium bowl and leave to stand for 2–3 minutes. Roughly chop the figs, place in a separate bowl and pour on just enough boiling water to cover. Set aside to soak.

2 Whisk the oil, remaining honey, eggs and egg yolk into the yeast mixture.

3 Mix the flour and salt in a large bowl, add the yeast mixture and stir with a wooden spoon until the dough comes together into a large, soft ball.

4 Turn the dough out onto a lightly floured surface and knead for 5–10 minutes (see page 12) until smooth. It should be soft, but not too sticky to knead.

5 Transfer the dough to a large, lightly oiled bowl, cover with lightly oiled cling film and set aside in a warm place until almost doubled in size, up to 2 hours.

6 Drain the soaked figs and pat dry with kitchen paper. Knock back the risen dough and knead in the figs until combined.

7 Divide the dough into 4 equal pieces. Roll and stretch each one into a rope about 30cm long. If any bits of the dried fruit fall out, just poke them back in with your finger.

8 To shape the loaf, arrange 2 strands in each direction, perpendicular to each other (like a noughts and crosses game). Weave them so that one side is over, and the other is under, where they meet (as shown). Take the 4 ropes that come from underneath the centre and move them over the rope to their right (as shown). Take those ropes that were on the right and again, move each rope over the rope before, this time to the left (as shown). If you have extra length to your ropes, you can repeat these left-right moves until you run out of rope. Tuck the corners under the dough with the sides of your hands to form a round loaf.

9 Transfer the shaped dough to a lightly oiled baking sheet, cover with lightly oiled cling film and leave to prove for about 45 minutes until nearly doubled in size again. Meanwhile, heat the oven to 190°C/gas mark 5.

10 Beat the egg for the glaze in a small bowl using a fork. Brush the risen loaf with the egg and sprinkle with the sugar. Bake in the middle of the oven for 40–45 minutes, or until the loaf is golden brown, sounds hollow when tapped on the base and feels light for its size. If it starts to take on a lot of colour in the oven, cover with a sheet of foil to finish cooking. Transfer to a wire rack to cool.

MALT LOAF

MAKES 2 small loaves

25g butter	400g plain flour
75g malt extract	1 tsp salt
2 tbsp black treacle	200g raisins
40g fresh yeast	Olive oil, to grease
170ml tepid water	Runny honey, to glaze

This malt loaf can be sliced and either toasted or eaten cold. Either way, spreading it with good, salty butter is a must! You will need two 450–500g loaf tins.

1 Melt the butter gently in a small pan, together with the malt extract and treacle, then leave to cool.

2 In a small bowl, dissolve the yeast in a little of the tepid water and set aside.

3 Sift the flour and salt into a bowl, then mix in the raisins.

4 Add the yeast, the cooled butter mix and most of the remaining water to the flour mixture. Mix to a soft dough, adding more water as required to make a soft dough, using some of the water to swill out the yeast bowl. Knead the dough for 10 minutes (see page 12) until smooth and elastic.

5 Oil the loaf tins. Divide the dough into 2 equal pieces and shape to fit the tins (see page 14). Cover with oiled cling film and leave to rise in a warm place until doubled in size and the dough feels soft and pillowy to the touch, leaving a shallow indent when pressed, 45–60 minutes. Meanwhile, heat the oven to 200°C/gas mark 6.

6 Bake the loaves in the centre of the oven for 30–35 minutes until brown on top and the loaves sound hollow when tapped on the underside.

7 Turn out the loaves onto a wire rack, brush with honey to glaze and leave to cool. Serve sliced and generously buttered.

ZOPF
(PLAITED BUTTER BREAD)

MAKES 1 large plaited loaf	
200ml milk	10g caster sugar
75g butter	7g fast-action dried yeast
425g strong white flour, plus extra to dust	2 eggs
10g salt, plus a pinch for the glaze	Oil, to grease

This is a version of a traditional Swiss enriched bread that has a rich golden colour when baked. Any leftover loaf can be made into a special bread and butter pudding or pain perdu.

1 Put the milk and butter in a saucepan and heat until the butter has melted and the milk is warm; the mixture should be tepid, about 38°C.

2 Mix the flour, salt, sugar and yeast in a large bowl and make a well in the centre. In a small bowl, lightly beat one of the eggs using a fork.

3 Pour the egg into the well along with three quarters of the milk and butter mixture. Mix to form a dough, adding as much of the remaining liquid as necessary to make a soft but not sticky dough.

4 Turn out onto a lightly floured surface and knead the dough for 10 minutes (see page 12) until smooth and elastic. Transfer the dough to a lightly oiled bowl and cover with lightly oiled cling film. Leave to rise for about 45 minutes–1 hour until doubled in size.

5 Knock back the risen dough for about 1 minute, then divide it into 3 equal pieces. Working fairly quickly so the dough does not over-prove, stretch and roll each piece into a rope, about 30cm long.

6 Place the 3 pieces of dough in an 'H' shape with the middle piece going under and over the 2 outer pieces. Plait one side from the middle towards you and then turn it over and plait the other side from the middle towards you again, to give an evenly plaited dough (as shown on page 28).

7 Place the plaited dough on a floured baking sheet, tuck the ends underneath and cover with lightly oiled cling film. Leave to prove for about 30 minutes, or until nearly doubled in size. Meanwhile, heat the oven to 220°C/gas mark 7.

8 In a small bowl, lightly beat the remaining egg with a fork, add the pinch of salt and sieve. Glaze the risen loaf carefully with the egg wash. Lower the oven setting to 200°C/gas mark 6 just before placing the loaf in the oven, and bake for 30–35 minutes until golden and sounding hollow when tapped underneath. Place on a wire rack to cool.

CHOCOLATE FOCACCIA

MAKES 1 large loaf	
10g fresh yeast	250g strong white flour,
30g caster sugar	plus extra to dust
150–160ml tepid water	1 tsp salt
50g dark chocolate	2 tbsp olive oil, plus extra
	to grease

This makes a delicious breakfast bread to serve with strong coffee or hot chocolate. The loaf only has one rise, so it has the characteristic uneven holes and rustic texture of a classic focaccia. Flavoured with dark chocolate, it is not overly sweet, though you could use a combination of dark and milk or even white chocolate for extra sweetness. You might like to try adding grated orange zest or chopped toasted hazelnuts to the dough too.

1 Put the yeast and sugar in a small bowl, add 2 tbsp of the tepid water and stir until the yeast and sugar have dissolved.

2 Chop the chocolate into roughly 1cm pieces.

3 Mix the flour and salt in a large bowl. Pour in the yeast liquid and 1 tbsp of the oil. Add three quarters of the remaining water, using some to swill out any yeast left in the bowl. Stir quickly, adding as much of the remaining water as you need to make a soft but not sticky dough, mixing well.

4 Transfer the dough to a lightly floured surface and knead for 2–3 minutes (see page 12) until slightly elastic and smooth. Do not be tempted to add more flour if you can possibly knead it without; the dough should be soft and a little wet. Gently knead in the chocolate pieces.

5 Shape the dough into a tight round or oval shape by pulling it around itself (see steps 1–3, page 14), then transfer to a lightly oiled baking sheet. Pat it lightly to flatten a little, making sure the chocolate pieces are not sticking out of the dough. Cover with lightly oiled cling film.

6 Place in a warm place and leave to rise for about 1–2 hours, or until doubled in size. Meanwhile, heat the oven to 200°C/ gas mark 6.

7 To check the dough has risen enough, lightly press it in towards the base with a finger; it should leave an indent. With lightly oiled fingers, make dimples at regular intervals over the surface of the dough, taking care not to push too hard and collapse the dough. Drizzle the remaining 1 tbsp oil over the top.

8 Bake in the oven for 20–30 minutes until golden. To test if it is cooked, turn the loaf over and tap the underside; it should sound hollow and feel somewhat light for its size. Remove from the oven and transfer to a wire rack to cool.

CRANBERRY AND PISTACHIO COURONNE

MAKES 1 large loaf

FOR THE DOUGH
150ml milk
15g butter
225g strong white flour,
    plus extra to dust
1 tsp salt
1½ tsp fast-action dried yeast
½ tsp caster sugar
1 egg
Oil, to grease

FOR THE FILLING
1 orange
100g dried cranberries
50g raisins
90g unsalted butter, softened
70g soft light brown sugar
30g plain flour
70g pistachio nuts

TO FINISH
60g smooth apricot jam
15g pistachio nuts, toasted

Bursting with cranberries and pistachios, this crown makes a wonderful centrepiece for a celebration, particularly at Christmas. You could even add some Christmas spices to the dough.

1 Pour the milk into a small saucepan and bring to scalding point (see page 155) over a medium heat. Add the butter to the milk, remove from the heat and leave the butter to melt and the mixture to cool to tepid, about 38°C.

2 For the filling, finely grate the orange zest and squeeze the juice. Put the dried cranberries and raisins in a small bowl, pour over the orange juice and set aside to soak.

3 For the dough, mix the flour and salt in a large bowl, stir in the yeast and caster sugar and make a well in the centre. Lightly beat the egg in a separate bowl.

4 Pour the egg and three quarters of the tepid milk and butter mixture into the well in the flour, and mix thoroughly with a wooden spoon until a soft but not sticky dough is formed. Add more liquid if necessary, or a little flour if it becomes too sticky.

5 Turn out the dough onto a lightly floured surface and knead for 10 minutes (see page 12) until elastic, smooth and shiny. Place in a lightly oiled bowl, cover with lightly oiled cling film and leave to rise until doubled in size, 1–2 hours.

6 Meanwhile, to make the filling, drain the cranberries and raisins and discard the juice. Cream the butter and brown sugar together in a bowl, using an electric whisk, until light and fluffy. Add the flour, pistachio nuts, raisins and cranberries, and orange zest and stir well to combine.

7 Turn out the risen dough onto a lightly floured surface and gently roll out into a rectangle about 35 x 25cm. Spread the filling over the dough and roll it up lengthways as you would a Swiss roll (as shown), making sure it is well sealed. Using a large floured knife, cut the roll in half lengthways leaving one end intact (as shown) to help with twisting the dough.

8 Twist both halved lengths together to form a rope and then join the ends to form a crown (couronne) shape (as shown). Carefully transfer this to a baking sheet lined with baking parchment. Cover with lightly oiled cling film and leave to prove until it has increased in size by half again, and when you press your finger lightly in the side, an indentation remains. Meanwhile, heat the oven to 200°C/gas mark 6.

9 Bake in the oven for 25–35 minutes until golden brown with no grey patches of uncooked dough. Transfer the couronne to a wire rack to cool.

10 To finish, melt the jam with a little water and brush over the loaf, then sprinkle over the pistachio nuts.

ROQUEFORT, SAUTERNES AND RAISIN BREAD

MAKES 1 large loaf

1 quantity brioche dough
(see page 106)
100g plump, golden raisins
100ml Sauternes or another
pale dessert wine

150g mascarpone cheese
170g Roquefort cheese
Butter, to grease
Flour, to dust
Freshly ground black pepper

This bread delivers compatible foods – bread, cheese, fruit and wine – all in one hit. The soft texture and buttery flavour of brioche dough is perfect for the fruit and cheese to sink into, though an enriched white bread dough (see page 25) also works well, for a less rich result. Simply tear the bread into chunks and serve with a plate of good charcuterie, such as Serrano or Bayonne ham, and a carafe of red wine.

1 Make the brioche dough following the recipe on page 106, up to the end of step 6.

2 While the dough is chilling, put the raisins and wine in a small saucepan over a low heat and slowly bring to the boil. Remove from the heat and leave to cool in the pan.

3 Put the mascarpone in a small bowl and season well with black pepper. Roughly crumble the Roquefort, discarding any rind. Heat the oven to 200°C/gas mark 6.

4 Grease a large baking tray generously with butter, then dust it lightly with flour. Place the brioche dough on the baking tray and, using a rolling pin or floured hands, roll or pat it out to a rough oval shape, about 24 x 20cm. The finished loaf should have a natural form, so there's no need to be too precise about the shape and size, just make sure it's big enough to hold the topping. Leave to relax for 15 minutes.

5 Dip the fingertips of one hand into a little flour to prevent them from sticking, and make deep indentations all over the surface of the dough, creating little pockets.

6 Spread the mascarpone over the dough, gently pushing it into the pockets and leaving a clear border of about 2cm all round.

7 Using a slotted spoon, remove the raisins from the pan, reserving the wine, and scatter them over the mascarpone, tucking them into the pockets where possible. Top the dough with the Roquefort, ensuring that it is evenly distributed, and spoon over the reserved wine. The topping will look quite wet at this stage, but the moisture will sink into the dough as it cooks, infusing it with flavour.

8 Bake in the top third of the oven for 20 minutes, then lower the oven setting to 180°C/gas mark 4 and continue to cook for a further 10–15 minutes until golden, cooked through and the topping is bubbling and just beginning to caramelise. Transfer to a wire rack and leave to cool slightly. Serve warm or at room temperature.

Variations

✱ Try other fruit and cheese combinations, such as dried or fresh figs with Gorgonzola, Medjool dates with dolcelatte, or thickly sliced, juicy peaches with salty feta.

CHEESE GANNAT

MAKES 1 medium loaf	
100ml milk	Pinch of English mustard
50g butter	powder
15g fresh yeast	2 eggs
2 tbsp tepid water	Oil, to grease
Pinch of caster sugar	100g strong hard cheese,
125g strong white flour, plus	such as Cheddar or
extra to dust	Gruyère
125g wholemeal flour	Milk, to glaze
1 tsp salt	Freshly ground black pepper
Pinch of cayenne pepper	

This is a delicious enriched cheese bread, a little like a savoury brioche. You will need a 20cm round cake tin, or moule à manqué.

1 Pour the milk into a small saucepan and bring to scalding point (see page 155) over a medium heat, then remove from the heat and leave to cool to tepid, about 38°C. Add the butter and leave to melt in the milk as it cools.

2 In a small bowl, mix the yeast with the water and sugar to create a loose paste.

3 Sift the flours, salt, cayenne and mustard powder into a bowl and grind in a little black pepper. Make a well in the centre of the flour. Beat the eggs in a small bowl, using a fork.

4 Pour the yeast mixture into the well, making sure no yeast is left behind. Add the beaten eggs and three quarters of the tepid milk and butter mixture, trying to ensure all the butter goes into the mixture. Stir with a cutlery knife, then with your fingers, adding enough of the reserved milk to make a soft but not sticky dough.

5 Transfer the dough to a lightly floured surface and knead for 8 minutes (see page 12) until smooth. (If the dough is very soft you can knead it in the bowl instead.) Place in a lightly oiled bowl, cover with lightly oiled cling film and leave in a warm place for about 1 hour until doubled in size.

6 Grate the cheese. Transfer the dough to the work surface and knock it back, kneading for 2–3 minutes and adding in all but a handful of the cheese as you knead. Lightly oil the cake tin.

7 Divide the dough into 8 equal pieces and shape each piece into a roll (see page 67). Arrange 7 buns around the edge of the prepared tin, leaving a little space between them, then place the eighth one in the middle. (The dough will expand and the buns will join together.)

8 Cover with lightly oiled cling film and leave to prove for 20–30 minutes until the dough has visibly risen (it will rise further while baking). Meanwhile, heat the oven to 200°C/gas mark 6.

9 Bake in the oven for 25–30 minutes, or until well risen and golden brown, and between the buns the dough is cooked and not at all grey. (If it starts to take on a lot of colour in the oven, cover with a sheet of greaseproof paper to finish cooking.)

10 Remove from the oven and brush the surface of the cooked buns with a little milk. Sprinkle with the reserved cheese and return to the oven for 5 minutes, or until the cheese is bubbling and starting to brown. Turn out onto a wire rack to cool.

6

YEASTED LAYERED DOUGHS

Here the skills of bread making and layered pastries come together to create tender, flaky pastries. The dough is rolled and folded with butter into hundreds of thin layers which then rise and separate – helped by the yeast in the dough and the heat of the oven.

We use a croissant base dough for all the pastries in this chapter, so by learning one technique you will be able to go on and bake a whole array of delicious pastries. The dough is incredibly versatile once mastered. Once you've savoured the smell of French pastries and croissants baking in your own home you'll be making them for a special treat time and again. They give a tremendous sense of satisfaction.

CROISSANT DOUGH

MAKES 1 quantity

500g strong white flour,
    plus extra to dust
1½ tsp salt
50g caster sugar
20g fresh yeast

125ml tepid water
1 small egg
125ml cold milk
Oil, to grease
200g cold, but pliable butter

The détrempe, or base dough, should ideally be made 12–24 hours in advance to let the flavours develop, and the fully prepared dough can be rested overnight before shaping and baking your croissants or pastries.

1 Mix the flour and salt in a large bowl and stir in the sugar. Mix the yeast with 60ml of the tepid water in a small bowl until dissolved. Mix the egg, remaining water and milk together and add to the flour along with the yeast mixture, to create a smooth dough that feels soft and slightly tacky.

2 Knead the dough lightly for about 6 minutes (see page 12) until smooth and slightly elastic.

3 Place the dough in a very lightly oiled, large plastic bag. Exclude all the air and tie a loose knot at the top. Leave the dough at room temperature for about 1 hour to ensure the yeast is working (the dough will increase in size), then place in the fridge for at least 6 hours, or overnight.

4 Take the dough from the fridge and remove from the plastic bag. On a lightly floured surface, reshape the dough into a ball, without working it excessively or it will become too elastic. Try to ensure there are no folds or holes in the ball of dough.

5 Using a sharp knife, cut a cross in the top, halfway through the dough.

6 Now stretch each corner of the cut dough away from the dough ball and roll into a thin flap. Place the butter between 2 sheets of baking parchment and lightly bash it using a rolling pin, to ensure it is pliable, but not greasy. When it is similar in consistency to the dough, shape it into a square (still in the parchment) the size of the centre of the dough.

7 Place the butter in the centre of the dough.

8 Fold over the flaps to encase the butter completely. This is important to stop the butter 'squidging' out of the dough.

9 Lightly re-flour the work surface. 'Ridge' and then roll the dough into a rectangle, 3 times as long as it is wide, and about 5–7.5mm thick. To do this, lightly tap the dough with a rolling pin over the entire surface, holding the rolling pin loosely in both hands, then turn the dough 90° and ridge again, then roll, until it has reached the correct size and thickness.

10 Neaten the sides and corners, brush off the excess flour and fold the dough into 3, so the bottom third folds up over the middle third and the top third comes down over the 2 layers.

11 Wrap in cling film and chill in the fridge for 15 minutes to rest, ensuring it has enough time to relax to prevent too much elasticity but checking the butter doesn't harden or it may break through the dough. Repeat steps 9, 10 and 11 until you have completed 3 'roll and folds', making sure that the folded edge is to the side before starting to ridge each time.

12 Roll the dough out into a large rectangle, 4mm thick, and chill for at least 4 hours, or overnight on a very lightly floured tray and covered with very lightly oiled cling film.

A note about the butter...

✱ To ensure the butter will be incorporated in fine, even layers it must be worked (step 6) until it is the pliable and able to be folded in on itself without cracking, but not greasy.

1 Checking the consistency of the dough after mixing: it should feel soft and slightly tacky.

2 Checking the texture of the dough after kneading lightly for 6 minutes: it should be smooth and slightly elastic.

3 Sealing the dough in a plastic bag to exclude all the air, ready for a light rise at room temperature before placing in the fridge.

4 Reshaping the rested dough, without over-working it.

(Continued overleaf)

5 Cutting a cross in the top of the dough, halfway through.

6 Stretching the 4 corners away and rolling them into thin flaps.

7 Placing the butter in the centre of the dough.

8 Folding the flaps of dough over the butter to encase it completely.

9 Ridging the dough into a rectangle, by lightly tapping it with a rolling pin over the entire surface, then rolling it. The dough is then turned 90°, ridged and rolled again, repeating until it has reached the correct size and thickness.

10 Folding the rectangle of dough into 3, bringing the bottom third up over the middle third, before folding the top third down over the 2 layers.

11 Giving the dough a quarter turn, so the folded edge is to the side, to complete the first of 3 'roll and folds'.

12 Rolling the dough out to a large rectangle, 4mm thick before chilling on a very lightly floured tray, covered with very lightly oiled cling film.

CROISSANTS

MAKES about 10

1 quantity croissant dough
   (see page 130)
Flour, to dust

FOR THE GLAZE
1 egg yolk
1 tbsp milk

It is true that making croissants from scratch is pretty time-consuming, but you don't need to get up before dawn to have them on the table for breakfast. Make the dough the day before in a leisurely fashion, then shape the croissants and prove them overnight in the fridge. The following morning, let them come back to room temperature as you wait for the oven to heat and bake them as you make the coffee! Perfect for a weekend breakfast.

1 To shape the croissants, on a lightly floured surface, use a large knife to trim the edges of the dough to a large rectangle, 4–5mm thick. Using a triangular template, 11cm across the base and 13cm measured vertically from the middle of the base to the top point, cut the dough into triangles.

2 Make a 7mm cut halfway along the shorter side of the triangle of dough.

3 Working with one triangle at a time with the longer point away from you, stretch out the 2 shorter points, then roll the triangle up from the short side.

4 The tip should fold over the top of the croissant and be tucked just underneath the croissant.

5 Place the shaped croissants on a baking sheet, spacing them well apart and either curving them into a crescent or leaving them straight.

6 Cover loosely with lightly oiled cling film and leave to prove in a cool place for about 50–80 minutes until puffed up. They mustn't warm up too much or the butter in the layers will melt, causing greasiness and a poor rise. Meanwhile, heat the oven to 210°C/gas mark 6½. When the croissants have puffed up and a small indentation remains when you press one gently with a finger towards the base, they are ready to be glazed and baked.

7 Beat the egg with the milk in a small bowl using a fork, then sieve it. Brush the croissants carefully with the glaze and bake in the top of the oven for 8–10 minutes, then lower the oven setting to 190°C/gas mark 5 and bake for a further 15–20 minutes, or until a deep golden brown, they feel light for their size and there are no grey, doughy patches. If they are becoming too brown in the oven, cover with greaseproof paper to continue cooking.

8 Remove the croissants from the oven and leave to cool on a wire rack.

TECHNIQUE
SHAPING CROISSANTS

Once you have your dough prepared and rested, it is relatively quick and easy to shape croissants. You will need a triangular template, measuring 11cm across the base and 13cm from the mid-point of the base to the top. Cut the template from a piece of card or rigid plastic, such as the lid of an ice-cream tub. Lay the chilled rectangle of dough on a lightly floured surface and trim the edges to neaten before you start.

1 Cutting the dough into triangles, using a template as a guide.

2 Making a small 7mm cut halfway along the short edge of the triangle.

3 Rolling up the triangle of dough from the short side.

(Continued overleaf)

4 Tucking the tip of the triangle underneath the croissant.

5 Placing the shaped croissants on a baking sheet, spacing them well apart and either curving them into a crescent or leaving them straight.

6 Covering the tray of croissants with lightly oiled cling film, ready for proving at room temperature.

7 Carefully brushing the proved croissants with egg glaze before baking.

HAM AND CHEESE CROISSANTS

MAKES 6	

1 quantity croissant dough (see page 130)
Flour, to dust

FOR THE FILLING
35g Gruyère cheese
15g Parmesan cheese
45g piece of smoked ham

15g butter
15g flour
100ml milk
¼ tsp Dijon mustard

FOR THE GLAZE
1 egg

Here the flavours of a classic croque monsieur are used in a savoury croissant filling. Delicious for brunches or picnic lunches.

1 Have the croissant dough ready, chilling it in the fridge for 10 minutes, or until firm, to make it easier to work with.

2 Grate the cheeses and cut the ham into 5mm cubes.

3 Melt the butter in a small saucepan over a low to medium heat, then stir in the flour. Cook for 1 minute, stirring well with a wooden spoon.

4 Remove from the heat and start to add the milk, a little at a time, stirring and incorporating it well as it is added to the roux. Once half of the milk has been incorporated, add the remaining milk in generous additions, and return the pan to the heat.

5 Increase the heat to medium to high and stir the sauce continuously as it comes to the boil, then reduce the heat and simmer for 2 minutes. Remove from the heat and add the cheeses, mustard and ham. Set aside to cool.

6 Place the chilled dough on a lightly floured surface and, using a large knife, trim the edges to make a large rectangle. Using a triangular template, 14cm across the base and 16cm measured vertically from the middle of the base to the top, cut the dough into triangles (as shown on page 135).

7 Put 1 tbsp of the cooled cheese sauce near the base of a triangle and flatten it slightly. Roll the dough over the sauce and shape into a croissant (see page 135). Repeat with the remaining triangles and sauce, placing the rolled croissants on a baking tray, spacing them well apart. Cover loosely with lightly oiled cling film and leave to prove in a cool place for about 50–80 minutes until doubled in size. Meanwhile, heat the oven to 220°C/gas mark 7.

8 Beat the egg in a small bowl using a fork, then sieve it. Brush the croissants with the egg glaze and bake in the oven for 8–10 minutes, then lower the oven setting to 190°C/gas mark 5 and bake for a further 15–20 minutes, or until an even deep golden colour. Cool on a wire rack.

CHERRY ALMOND CROISSANTS

| MAKES 8 |

8 croissants

FOR THE SYRUP
6 tbsp granulated sugar
60ml Kirsch, rum or orange
    juice
60ml water
100g dried cherries

FOR THE ALMOND FILLING
125g butter, softened
125g caster sugar
1 egg, plus 1 extra yolk
125g ground almonds
1 tbsp plain flour
½ tsp vanilla extract
2 drops of almond extract

TO FINISH
3 tbsp flaked almonds
Icing sugar, to dust

This recipe is a good way to use up day-old croissants. The syrup adds moisture, as does the almond filling.

1 To make the syrup, put the sugar and Kirsch, rum or orange juice in a small pan with the water and dried cherries and heat gently, stirring, until the sugar has dissolved. Increase the heat and simmer for 1 minute, then remove from the heat and leave to cool.

2 Heat the oven to 190°C/gas mark 5. Cut the croissants in half horizontally and set aside.

3 To make the almond filling, cream together the butter and sugar using an electric whisk until pale, then beat in the egg and extra yolk. Stir in the ground almonds and flour, then add the vanilla and almond extracts and mix to a smooth paste. Set aside 2 tbsp for the top of the croissants.

4 Drain the dried cherries in a small sieve over a bowl, pressing the fruit with the back of a spoon to extract as much syrup as possible, then stir the cherries into the almond filling.

5 Brush the cut sides of the croissant halves with the syrup, then divide the cherry and almond filling between the croissant bases. Spread it using a cutlery knife and sandwich with the top half of each croissant. Spread a little of the reserved almond cream over the top of each croissant, then sprinkle with flaked almonds, pressing them down gently so that they stick.

6 Transfer the croissants to a baking sheet and bake in the oven for 15–20 minutes, or until the frangipane has set and the almonds on top are golden brown.

7 Serve warm or at room temperature, with a little icing sugar sifted over the top.

PAIN AU CHOCOLAT

MAKES about 8

1 quantity croissant dough
  (see page 130)
160g good quality dark
  chocolate (minimum 60%
  cocoa solids)

FOR THE GLAZE
1 egg yolk
1 tbsp milk

We find that the basic croissant dough makes perfect pain au chocolat. It has just the right flakiness and buttery flavour. Try adding 1 tsp of marmalade along with the chocolate inside each pastry for a hint of chocolate orange flavour.

1 Have the croissant dough prepared and ready.

2 Using a large knife, trim the dough to a large rectangle and cut into smaller rectangles, about 15 x 10cm.

3 Lay 10g chocolate across the middle of each rectangle (as shown) and fold one side of the pastry over the chocolate, then place another 10g of chocolate across the middle of the dough and fold the remaining side of the dough over the second chocolate (as shown), like a letter. Turn the filled pastry over so the fold is underneath and place on a baking sheet. Space the pastries well apart to allow room for rising.

4 Cover loosely with lightly oiled cling film and leave to prove in a cool place for 50–80 minutes until puffed up. They mustn't warm up too much or the butter in the layers will melt, causing greasiness and a poor rise.

5 Meanwhile, heat the oven to 210°C/gas mark 6½. When the pastries have puffed up and a small indentation remains when you press one gently with a finger at the base, they are ready to be glazed and baked. For the glaze, beat the egg yolk and milk lightly together in a small bowl, then sieve it.

6 Brush the pastries carefully with the glaze. Bake in the hottest part of the oven for 8–10 minutes, then lower the oven setting to 190°C/gas mark 5 and bake for a further 15–20 minutes, or until a deep golden brown. If they are becoming too brown, cover with greaseproof paper to continue cooking.

7 Remove from the oven and cool on a wire rack.

A note about trimmings...

✳ Don't throw away the trimmings from the dough; they can be layered up, re-rolled and folded. They will give a slightly less uniform rise but otherwise will be fine.

PAIN AU RAISINS

MAKES 8–10

1 quantity croissant dough
   (see page 130)
100g raisins
50ml rum or brandy
100ml warm water
1 egg

½ quantity crème pâtissière
   (made with an extra 1 tbsp
   sugar, see page 152)
Sugar syrup (see page 152),
   to glaze

These raisin spiral buns are made with a basic croissant dough for a flaky, buttery texture, but they are also very good made with the same quantity of brioche dough (see page 106) for a more 'cakey' texture. Make the crème pâtissière (as well as the dough) the day before you are shaping the pain au raisin to make the assembly more relaxed.

1 Have the croissant dough prepared and ready.

2 Put the raisins in a small bowl. Mix the rum or brandy with the water, pour over the raisins and leave to soak for 1–2 hours. Lightly beat the egg in a small bowl with a fork and set aside.

3 Using a large knife, trim the dough to a large rectangle, about 5mm thick, and spread the crème pâtissière evenly over the dough. Drain the raisins and scatter them evenly over the crème pâtissière (as shown).

4 Starting from the narrower end, roll the dough up into a thick roll, brushing a little of the beaten egg across the end of the dough before finishing rolling to seal the edge (as shown).

5 Trim off the ends of the roll using a large, sharp knife, then cut the roll into 2cm slices. Place these cut side up on a baking tray and flatten them a little with your fingers (as shown).

6 Cover loosely with lightly oiled cling film and leave to prove in a cool place for 50–80 minutes until puffed up. They mustn't warm up too much or the butter in the layers will melt, causing greasiness and a poor rise.

7 Meanwhile, heat the oven to 210°C/gas mark 6½. When the pastries have puffed up and a small indentation remains when you press one gently with a finger at the base, they are ready to be glazed with beaten egg and baked.

8 Brush the top of the pastries carefully with the beaten egg. Bake in the top of the oven for 8–10 minutes, then lower the oven setting to 190°C/gas mark 5 and bake for a further 15–20 minutes, or until a deep golden brown. If they appear to be browning too quickly, cover with greaseproof paper and continue cooking.

9 Remove from the oven, brush carefully with the sugar syrup to glaze and cool on a wire rack.

DANISH PASTRIES

MAKES 6–8

1 quantity croissant dough
   (see page 130)

FOR THE FILLINGS
1 quantity frangipane
   (see page 153)
1 quantity crème pâtissière
   (see page 152)

CINNAMON BUTTER
60g butter
60g caster sugar
2 tsp ground cinnamon

FOR THE GLAZE
1 egg yolk
1 tbsp milk

TO FINISH
1 quantity glacé icing
   (see page 153)

. . . .

You can be really creative with Danish pastries – both in terms of flavourings and shapes. They can be filled with spiced butters, frangipane or crème pâtissière along with dried or poached fruit. Try poached rhubarb, pears or plums in a diamond pastry (see page 148), or frangipane and dried fruits in a comb (see page 147) or pinwheel (see page 146).

1 Have the croissant dough and fillings prepared and ready.

2 For the cinnamon butter, mix the butter, sugar and cinnamon together in a small bowl until well combined.

3 For the glaze, beat the egg yolk and milk together lightly in a small bowl, then sieve it. Shape the pastries into wheels, squares, pinwheels, combs and/or diamonds as described and shown on pages 145–9.

4 Place the pastries on a baking sheet, spacing them well apart to allow for rising. Cover loosely with lightly oiled cling film and leave to prove in a cool place for 50–80 minutes until doubled in size. Meanwhile, heat the oven to 220°C/gas mark 7.

5 Carefully brush the pastries with the glaze. Bake in the oven for 8–10 minutes, then lower the oven setting to 190°C/gas mark 5 and continue to cook for a further 15–20 minutes until an even deep golden brown. Transfer to a wire rack and leave to cool completely.

6 Once cold, drizzle or spoon the glacé icing on top of the pastries. Allow to set before serving.

SHAPING CINNAMON WHEELS

Using a large knife, trim the dough to a large rectangle. Spread the cinnamon butter over the rolled out pastry, leaving a 1cm border around the edge. Roll from the narrow end into a thick roll, sealing the end with a little egg glaze. Chill, covered, if the pastry is very soft to firm up, then trim off the edges and cut into 2–3cm slices. Turn cut side up and flatten them a little using your fingers.

SHAPING ALMOND SQUARES

Cut the pastry into 12–15cm squares. Place 1 tsp frangipane in the centre of each square and fold each of the corners over so each tip sits on top of the frangipane. Press down slightly to seal the corners together.

SHAPING
PINWHEELS

1 Cut the pastry into 12–15cm squares. From each corner of each square make a cut towards the centre about 3cm long.

2 Place 1 tsp frangipane in the uncut centre of each square. Take one of the points of the pastry, fold it into the middle and press onto the frangipane to secure.

3 Continue to fold alternate points of pastry (one from each corner) into the middle and press to secure. This leaves one unfolded point at each corner and the pastry should now resemble a pinwheel.

SHAPING COMBS

1 Cut the pastry into 10cm squares and place a line of either frangipane or cinnamon butter along the middle of each square. Brush the furthest edge with egg glaze, then fold the bottom half up over the filling to meet the other half squarely. Press the edges to seal; the sealed area should be at least 1.5–2cm wide.

2 Cut through the sealed edge of the dough only as far as the start of the filling, at 1cm intervals.

3 Carefully bend the filled side inwards into a crescent shape, causing the comb teeth to spread a little.

SHAPING
DIAMONDS

....

1 Cut the pastry into 12–15cm squares, then 1cm in from the edge across opposing corners, cut through the pastry almost to the next corner on both sides.

2 Place 1 tsp frangipane or cinnamon butter in the centre of the pastry and lift the outer cut border over the filling to sit on top of the opposing inner corner.

3 Now lift the opposite outer cut border over the filling to sit on top of the opposing inner corner.

PECAN AND MAPLE PASTRIES

MAKES 8

1 quantity croissant dough
  (see page 130)

1–2 tbsp maple syrup
50g pecan nuts

FOR THE FILLING
85g butter, softened
85g soft dark brown sugar

FOR THE GLAZE
1 egg

These pastries have a delicious, almost fudgy nut sugar filling. For a decorative finish, drizzle the cooled pastries with glacé icing (see page 153) and sprinkle with chopped toasted pecans.

1 Have the croissant dough ready, chilling it in the fridge for 10–15 minutes, or until it is firm and easy to work with.

2 For the filling, put the butter in a bowl and beat in the sugar and maple syrup, using a wooden spoon. Coarsely chop the pecan nuts and add them to the butter mixture. Place the filling in a piping bag fitted with a large plain nozzle big enough for the pecan pieces to go through. Alternatively, shape the filling into a log about 10cm in diameter and 16cm long on a piece of cling film, wrap with the cling film and chill until firm.

3 Roll out the dough to a 5mm thickness and cut into 12 x 8cm rectangles. Score a line, just deep enough to leave a mark but without cutting through the dough, 4cm in from each short side of the rectangles, to mark the rectangle into 3 equal sections.

4 Make parallel cuts, right through the dough, on a slight diagonal and about 1cm apart, along the outer sections of each square, abutting against the marks previously made and making sure the cuts reach the line you have marked but no further. The squares should now have what looks like the teeth of a comb on either side of an uncut central piece of dough.

5 Pipe the pecan butter down the middle of each square between the 2 rows of cuts, or cut the chilled butter into eight 10 x 2cm lengths and place a piece down the middle of the pastry between the 2 rows of cuts. Beat the egg in a small bowl using a fork and sieve it.

6 Working on one square at a time, carefully separate the 'teeth' on either sides of the filling and fold the strips of pastry from alternate sides over the top of the pecan butter to form a plaited lattice on the top. Ensure the lattice is fairly tight over the filling and seal each 'overlap' by brushing on a little of the beaten egg.

7 Place the pastries on a baking sheet, spacing them well apart to allow for rising. Cover with lightly oiled cling film and leave to prove in a cool place for 50–80 minutes until doubled in size. Meanwhile, heat the oven to 220°C/gas mark 7.

8 Carefully brush a little beaten egg over the proved pastries to glaze. Bake in the oven for 8–10 minutes, then lower the oven setting to 190°C/gas mark 5 and cook for a further 15–20 minutes until deep golden brown. Transfer to a wire rack and leave to cool completely.

CRÈME PÂTISSIÈRE

MAKES 1 quantity	
300ml milk	20g plain flour
3 egg yolks	20g cornflour
60g caster sugar	Few drops of vanilla extract

This is the thick custard, or pastry cream used to fill a variety of classic cakes, pastries and desserts. It can also be flavoured with coffee or chocolate.

1 Pour the milk into a small saucepan and bring to scalding point (see page 155) over a medium heat.

2 In a bowl, cream the egg yolks with the sugar and a little of the scalded milk to loosen the mixture, then sift in the flours and stir well to combine.

3 Gradually pour the remaining scalded milk onto the creamed mix, stirring well to keep the mixture smooth.

4 Return the mixture to the rinsed out pan and bring slowly to the boil, stirring continuously with a wooden spoon as it becomes thick; vigorously beat out any lumps if necessary. Simmer for 2 minutes, then allow to cool slightly and add vanilla extract to taste.

SUGAR SYRUP

MAKES about 500ml	
250g granulated sugar	500ml water

This is the basic 'stock' syrup used for fruit salads, poaching fruit, and in patisserie. It can be flavoured with a vanilla pod and, or other spices as required.

1 Put the sugar and water in a medium saucepan. Place over a low heat to dissolve the sugar, using the handle of a wooden spoon to gently agitate it and prevent it from 'caking' on the bottom of the pan. Avoid splashing the syrup up the sides of the saucepan.

2 Once the sugar has dissolved, use a pastry brush dipped in water to brush down the sides of the pan, to wash any remaining sugar crystals down into the syrup.

3 Increase the heat and do not stir from this point. Bring the syrup to the boil and boil steadily for 5 minutes. Take off the heat, cool and keep covered until needed.

FRANGIPANE

MAKES 1 quantity

100g butter
100g caster sugar
1 egg, plus 1 extra yolk, at
    room temperature

100g ground almonds
2 tbsp plain flour

This is the classic almond filling used for pastries and tarts. For optimum flavour, grind your own almonds in a food processor (with a little sugar to help break them down), but be careful not to over-grind the nuts or they will become greasy.

1 Cream the butter and sugar together in a bowl until well combined.

2 Beat the egg and yolk together, then gradually add to the creamed mixture, beating well between additions. Finally, stir in the ground almonds and flour until well combined.

GLACÉ ICING

MAKES 1 quantity

100g icing sugar

1–2 tbsp warm water

This simple icing is used as a decorative finish for pastries and enriched sweet breads. Add the liquid very slowly to achieve the desired consistency, or you will find you have to add more and more icing sugar. It is easy to end up with twice as much icing as you actually need this way!

1 Sift the icing sugar into a medium bowl.

2 Add small amounts of water while mixing well to ensure there are no lumps, until the icing reaches a consistency that can be poured but will hold its shape as it dries.

EQUIPMENT

Equipment

Trays and tins for baking do not need to be non-stick, but should be solid enough not to warp when they are heated.

Scales A set of good scales is important – electronic scales are more accurate when measuring smaller quantities

Chopping boards Use separate board for raw and cooked foods

Bowls A selection of various sizes, glass or stainless steel

Measuring jug

Juicer

Loaf tin 450–500g, 900g–1kg

Cake tins 20cm, 22cm and 24cm deep round cake tins

Moule a manqué Tin with sloping sides

Muffin tins

Casserole 23–25cm Le Crueset-style deep casserole

Baking sheets Some flat, some lipped

Shallow baking tins Selection of sizes

Roasting tins Selection of sizes

Proving baskets

Wire cooling racks

Oven gloves

Utensils

Good kitchen tools make work in the kitchen easier and more efficient. The following are particularly useful when baking breads and pastries:

Measuring spoons

Wooden spoons

Rolling pin

Kitchen scissors (a sturdy pair)

Swivel vegetable peeler

Apple corer

Pastry cutters

Pastry brush

Cutlery knife For mixing pastry

Palette knife

Spatula (heat resistant)

Dough scraper

Fine grater

Zester

Pans

Saucepans (at least 3 in a range of sizes from 18–28cm)

Frying pans (at least 2 in different sizes, from 16–28cm)

Knives

Large cook's knife Important for fine slicing, fine chopping and many other food preparation tasks

Paring knife For controlled cutting of small ingredients

Pastry knife A long serrated knife is used for cutting breads and pastries without crumbling or tearing

Small serrated knife This is very useful for preparing fruit

Small electrical equipment

Electric mixer A free-standing mixer with a dough hook is most useful for mixing and kneading doughs

Hand-held electric whisk Creams together butter and sugar very swiftly

Blender, hand-held stick blender, food processor Useful for purées and grinding nuts

Paper/lining products

Greaseproof paper

Baking parchment/silicone paper

Aluminium foil

Cling film

Non-stick baking mats (re-usable)

GLOSSARY

BLOOD TEMPERATURE 37–38°C: at this temperature a liquid feels neither hot nor cold to the touch; i.e. it is tepid.

BOIL To cook food submerged in liquid heated so that the bubbles are constant and vigorous.

BROWN To bake (or roast or fry) to achieve colour and flavour as the natural sugars caramelise, such as the surface of a bread.

CARAMEL Sugar turned to a deep terracotta brown by heating.

CARAMELISE See Brown (above).

CHILL To cool food down in the fridge or using an ice bath, ideally to 4°C.

CLARIFIED BUTTER Butter which has been heated and the milk solids removed. This gives it a clear appearance and allows it to be heated to a high temperature without burning, while retaining the flavour of butter.

CREAM To beat together ingredients in order to incorporate air, typically butter and sugar for a cake mixture.

EGG WASH Beaten egg (or beaten egg mixed with a little milk), sometimes salted, brushed onto pastry or bread to give it colour and shine once baked.

FINISH To complete a dish by adjusting its consistency, flavourings, seasoning and/or applying a garnish or decoration.

FOLD To combine two or more mixtures using a large metal spoon or spatula and a lifting and turning motion to avoid destroying the air bubbles. Usually one of the mixtures is more airy and delicate than the other.

GLAZE To lend a glossy finish. A glaze may be applied before or after cooking. For example, an egg glaze is applied to bread or pastry prior to baking, while runny honey or a sugar syrup may be brushed over warm pastries on removing from the oven.

KNEAD To work a bread dough vigorously in order to develop the gluten and elasticity for the correct texture.

KNOCK BACK OR KNOCK DOWN To knead or punch the air out of a risen bread dough so that when it rises for the second time it will have a finer, even texture.

LOOSEN When combining whisked egg whites into a heavier mixture, to first stir in a spoonful of the whisked whites to lighten the mixture before folding in the remainder.

OVEN SPRING The crack along the length of a loaf that is created by the yeast's final activity in the oven before it is killed by the intense heat.

PASS To push a purée or soft ingredients through a sieve to achieve a fine texture.

PINCH An approximate quantity that can be pinched between the thumb and forefinger, less than ⅛ tsp.

PITH The soft white layer directly beneath the coloured zest of citrus fruit. It is invariably bitter in flavour and avoided when zesting the fruit.

POACH To completely submerge food in liquid that is hot yet barely trembling (certainly not bubbling), either on the hob or in the oven. Ideal for cooking delicate food.

PROVE The final rise of a bread dough after it has been knocked back.

PURÉE Usually vegetables or fruit, blended and/or sieved until smooth. Purées can also be made from meat and fish.

REDUCE To rapidly boil a liquid in order to concentrate the flavour by evaporating some of the liquid.

RELAX OR REST To set pastry aside in a cool place, usually the fridge, to allow the gluten to relax before baking. This helps to minimise shrinking in the oven. Batters are also left to rest before use to allow the starch cells to swell, which results in a lighter cooked result.

ROAST To cook uncovered, without added liquid, in the oven.

RUB IN To rub small pieces of butter into flour with the fingertips until the mixture resembles breadcrumbs.

SCALD To heat a liquid (milk, usually) until on the verge of boiling. At scalding point, steam is escaping and bubbles are starting to form around the edge of the pan.

SCORE To make shallow or deep cuts in the surface of food with a sharp knife. For example, deeply scoring bread to create decorative slashes that open out on baking.

SEASON Usually simply to flavour with salt and pepper, but it can also involve adjusting acidity with lemon juice or sweetness by adding sugar. The term also describes rubbing a pan with oil and salt to make it non-stick.

SIMMER To cook food submerged in liquid, heated to a level that ensures small bubbles constantly appear around the edge of the pan.

SLAKE To mix a thickening ingredient such as cornflour with a little cold water and then whisk the mixture into the sauce to thicken it. Unstable ingredients such as yoghurt should also be slaked into a mixture using a little of the sauce, to prevent curdling.

SPONGE Fresh yeast is described as sponging if it is mixed with a little warm water and left until the yeast is seen to be working and frothing.

SWEAT To cook food gently in a little butter or oil, usually in a covered pan, to soften but not brown and release some of the moisture and natural sweetness.

SYRUPY The consistency of a sauce reduced down until it just coats the back of a spoon. Similar to warm syrup or honey.

WELL A hollow in a mound of flour in a bowl or on the work surface, created to contain the liquid ingredients before they are incorporated. Used in batter making.

ZEST The coloured outer skin of citrus fruit used for flavouring, which must be carefully removed from the bitter white pith before it is added. 'To zest' describes the action of finely paring the zest.

INDEX

ACKNOWLEDGEMENTS

The recipes in this book have been compiled, adapted and edited by Jenny Stringer, Claire Macdonald and Camilla Schneideman, but the authors are a large collection of Leiths staff and visiting teachers, past and present. Thank you to everyone who wrote recipes for this book, notably: Fiona Burrell, Louisa Bradford, Max Clark, Sarah Hall, Rupert Holden, Caroline Jones, Claire Macdonald, Heli Miles, Shenley Moore, Adriana Rabinovich, Camilla Schneideman, Belinda Spinney, Jenny Stringer and Ron Sweetser.

But with the sheer number of talented cooks around us at the school, we must say a big thank you to everyone who has helped develop ideas for this book, tested the recipes (particularly Sarah Hall who undertook an intensive testing programme!) and given valuable feedback during the tasting sessions. Special thanks must go to Helene Robinson-Moltke, Ansobe Smal and Belinda Spinney who were at the photo shoots.

Thank you to the team at Quadrille. We have been extremely lucky to continue our relationship with our editor Janet Illsley. Janet's patience with the authors is legendary – deadlines with this number of people involved required military organisation and, as ever, we are incredibly grateful for her wisdom. Thank you too Sally Somers for editing the copy.

Thank you to the team that worked together on the design and photography for this book: Peter Cassidy for his brilliant photography, Gabriella Le Grazie for her art direction, and Emily Kydd and Emily Quah (both Leiths graduates) for the food styling. We are thrilled with the new style Katherine Keeble has created for this series of books, so thank you all.

CREATIVE DIRECTOR Helen Lewis
PROJECT EDITOR Janet Illsley
DESIGN Katherine Keeble
ART DIRECTION Gabriella Le Grazie
PHOTOGRAPHER Peter Cassidy
FOOD STYLISTS Emily Kydd and Emily Quah
LEITHS CONSULTANTS Claire Macdonald, Helene Robinson-Moltke, Ansobe Smal and Belinda Spinney
COPY EDITOR Sally Somers
PROPS STYLISTS Iris Bromet and Cynthia Inions
PRODUCTION Vincent Smith, Tom Moore

First published in 2015 by
Quadrille Publishing Limited
www.quadrille.co.uk

Cataloguing in Publication Data: a catalogue record for this book is available from the British Library.

ISBN 978 184949 5486

Printed in China